CLOCK WORKS

JULIET BAWDEN

PHOTOGRAPHS BY JAMES DUNCAN

Trafalgar Square Publishing

FOR CLARE AND TIM FRANKL-BERTRAM

First published in the United States of America in 1995 by
Trafalgar Square Publishing
North Pomfret
Vermont 05053

Conceived and produced by
Anness Publishing Ltd
Boundary Row Studios
1 Boundary Row
London SE1 8HP

ISBN 1-57076-013-6

Library of Congress Catalog Card No: 94-60756

Editorial Director: Joanna Lorenz
Editorial Manager: Helen Sudell
Designer: Bobbie Colgate-Stone
Photography: James Duncan
Illustrations: John Hutchinson, Vana Haggerty

Printed and bound in Hong Kong

PUBLISHER'S NOTE
Crafts and hobbies are great fun to learn and can fill many rewarding hours of leisure
time, but some general points should be remembered for safety and care of the environment.
• Always use non-toxic materials, for example paints, glues and varnishes. If this is
not possible, always use materials in a well-ventilated area and always follow manufacturer's instructions.
• Craft knives, needles, scissors and all sharp instruments should be used with care.
Always use a cutting board or mat to avoid damage to household surfaces (it is also
safer to cut onto a firm, non-slip surface).
• Protect surfaces from paint, glue and varnish splashes by laying down old newspapers, plastic sheeting or an old sheet.

SOME USEFUL TERMS

UK	US
sticky tape	cellophane tape
cartridge paper	construction paper
card	posterboard
cord	string
PVA glue	white glue

CONTENTS

A HISTORY OF TIME

EARLY MAN HAD LITTLE NEED for mechanical clocks; he would wake at sunrise and go to bed at sunset. With the growth of civilization, man, at least in highly developed societies, began to feel the need for a means of measuring time.

In approximately 3500 BC, the early Egyptians divided the day and night into 12 hours each; at this time, the length of the hours depended on the seasons of the year. It was not until 3000 BC that the Babylonians regularized the hours by making them all the same length of time. The Romans then devised a calendar which had 10 lunar months which began on 1 March. However as this still meant that the year fell short, a special month was then intercalated between February 23rd and 24th. In 46 BC Julius Caesar commissioned the Greek astronomer Sosigenes to devise a new calendar which was based on the solar year, with 365 days for three consecutive years and an extra day added to the shortest month every fourth year: the leap year as we now know it.

Roman sun dial from Utica, Tunisia.

In Summer at the mouth of the River Tigris, the Egyptians built great calendar clocks of large stone blocks, similar to the circular arrangement that remains at Stonehenge in Britain; it is thought that Stonehenge was used to tell the time and was probably also used as a form of observatory. Later, sundials closer to today's model were introduced.

Later developments include a small, portable wooden shadow clock which consisted of a horizontal bar with a raised crosspiece at one end. The shadow would progress along the bar as the sun rose so the clock had to be positioned facing east in the morning and west in the afternoon.

The first clocks to calculate the full 24

An early 18th-century engraving of Stonehenge by Johannes Kip.

hours were also Egyptian. These were water clocks which worked on a principal similar to that of the trickling sand egg timer. Water trickled from one level to another through a hole into a bowl which was marked with the hours. This was particularly useful at night when the shadow clocks could not function. When the Egyptians discovered that sand could be used instead of water, the hour glass was born; it was used as a popular method of timekeeping up until the late sixteenth century, and the British Royal Navy continued to keep time using hour glasses until 1820.

Another method of timekeeping was to use thick candles marked into regular sections. Monks in newly Christian Britain timed their devotions by candle and were summoned to prayer by bells. King Alfred the Great also used candles to calculate time, each one burning for four hours. A number of Anglo-Saxon sundials still exist, high up on church walls or preserved in museums. The sun was an all-important symbol and any movement or change (such as an eclipse) was most significant. A priest who could foretell events relating to the sun was both useful and powerful. In some sophisticated religions, keeping to timetables of prayer became essential, and great effort was put into means of telling the time accurately.

In the eleventh century, the great cathedrals and abbeys of Europe kept a timekeeper who watched a sun dial and turned an hour glass. On each hour he would strike a bell to tell the monks to go to prayer. In the thirteenth century a new type of weight-driven clock first appeared which made timekeepers redundant.

In the fourteenth century, French and British monks devised a set of gear wheels controlled by balance, which were connected to a weight driving a

An early Egyptian depsydra or water clock. Time is measured as the bowl slowly fills with water.

This 14th-century manuscript depicts Richard of Wallingford, Abbot of St Albans and inventor of the astronomical clock.

An early weight-driven Pendulum Clock designed by Christian Huygens and built by Johannes van Ceulen.

pointer around a dial marked with the hours. The idea became popular and was further refined by the addition of striking mechanisms. Clocks at this time were for public use, and were large, heavy and made of iron. The skills used to manufacture these clocks were those of the blacksmith and later of the gunsmith. The domestic clock first appeared in the sixteenth century with brass replacing the iron and using small threaded screws, nuts and bolts.

Galileo had worked out the principle of the pendulum by 1585 but it was another hundred years before it was adopted for general use by clockmakers, most notably Salomon Coster, an eminent Dutchman who worked with the Dutch mathematician Christian Huygens. They achieved their first pendulum clock in 1657. By the eighteenth century the Royal Navy badly needed a clock which would allow them to calculate longitude at sea; in 1714 the British Admiralty offered a prize of £20,000 for a clock which was accurate enough to be only one degree out after a voyage from England to the West Indies and back. The prize was won by John Harrison (1693 – 1776) who, assisted by his brother, spent 40 years devising an accurate sea clock. He received his prize, aged 80,

The first spring-driven clock by Joseph Zeck.

A 17th-century hanging ball time piece by Jacobus Mayr.

The famous clock at Greenwich Observatory, designed by Thomas Tompion.

but it was to be other men who would transform Harrison's invention into a practical proposition, simplifying its production, so that it could be mass produced without losing its accuracy. Sea clocks are now known as chronometers.

In 1675 the Observatory at Greenwich was established and was used by King Charles II to study astronomy and navigation. Before 1880, when the British parliament passed an act making Greenwich time standard in the British Isles, clocks were inaccurate and people tended to use local sunrise and dusk times by which to set the time; this resulted in time being different from city to city. Some enterprising characters took advantage of the desire for standardization and accuracy: a John Beville travelled to Greenwich three times a week to set his watch and, on his return home, would sell the time to customers. When he died, the practice was continued by his daughter Ruth. In 1859 Big Ben was built outside the Houses of Parliament in London and Londoners would use it to tell the time. Those outside London had to make do with telegraph links between railway stations and post offices.

The greatest English clockmaker was Thomas Tompion (1673 – 1713). He specialized in bracket clocks encased in ebony and other fashionable woods. The dials were sometimes square or, later, arched. These were known as mantel clocks. The long case or grandfather clock was also perfected by Tompion and was immediately

A fine example of an early 17th-century German Diptych sundial, made from ivory and gilt brass.

Late 18th-century sundial cube by D. Beringer.

popular. The case testified to the cabinet maker's skills while the dial gave scope to the art of the enameller.

The first American clocks were those brought over by the early settlers, but as more and more craftsmen arrived it meant that the skills for making clocks were available locally. By the early eighteenth century clock making was established in New York, New England, Virginia and Pennsylvania.

The method of clock construction in America was similar to those used in England. However due to shortages of some materials such as brass, wood was often used as a substitute. Sometimes only the cases of the clocks were made locally, the movements and dials being imported and fitted to the manufactured cases.

Until the War of Independence only a small number of longcase clocks were produced but by the nineteenth century smaller mass produced clocks began to appear. Eli Terry of Massachusetts is credited with the first real mass production of clocks when in 1806 he made 4000 of them.

Following the War of Independence there was a rapid demand for cheaper and smaller clocks rather than the long case clock. Immigrant clock makers from Germany, the Netherlands and England met these needs by devising ways of producing clocks which could be manufactured using factory techniques as opposed to hand crafting. Makers involved in early factory production were Seth Thomas, Simon Willard and Chauncey Jerome.

During the nineteenth century many interesting developments took place in clock design including the production of a number of novelty clocks.

One such clock was a curvaceous shaped clock known as 'the acorn' clock, produced by J C Brown's Forestville MFG Company in Bristol, Connecticut. Always an innovator, Brown produced many different case styles such as ripple-front beehives and steeples.

Miniature bracket clock with a blue steel and gilt metal case by Thomas Tompion.

The acorn was unusual as it was made from laminated wood, which was employed to achieve the curved, acorn shape, sides of the case and the sidearm.

Another interesting clock was pioneered by Joseph Ives of Bristol, Connecticut around 1825-30. The 'Wagon Clock' was driven by a large leaf spring at its base which, being flexed at either end, gave the clock its motive power and resembled a spring of a wagon. Ives's clocks were of eight days duration whilst others might go for as long as a month or only for a day.

During the second half of the nineteenth century the calendar clock became an important item of production in clock manufacturing. It is believed that the first American clock-operated calendar was patented in 1953 by an Ithica inventor by the name of J H Hawes, although this calendar was not perpetual as it did not adjust for leap years. This adjustment came later in the hands of two other inventors named James E and Eugene M Mix. The Mix brothers improved on the mechanism and took out a patent in 1860 which was later purchased by the Seth Thomas clock company.

As more manufacturers began to produce shelf clocks the competition became very fierce and finer and more decorative features were added to achieve sales. Carved designs and fancy tablets became increasingly prominent. One such clock was the 'Triple Decker' shelf clock produced by the Dyer and Wadsworth company in Augusta, Georgia. It comprised three doors with carving and gilded columns and a brass eight-day movement made by Brige, Mallory and Company.

Mechanically operated clocks, the world over, are much the same now as they were one hundred years ago. The invention of the quartz mechanism has revolutionized the recording of time and is now more accurate and cheaper than ever. For a very small sum of money it is possible to buy a mechanism and produce your own clock. I hope the clock designs in this book inspire you to create your own personalized clock.

Left: A classic walnut marquetry longcase clock by Daniel Quare.

MAKING TIME: CLOCKS TO CREATE

THE SKILLS of the traditional clockmakers, or horologists, take seven years to acquire, the same training as for a vet or an architect. This book shows that beautiful clocks can be created simply, without special skills, using that modern and inexpensive invention, the quartz movement. Simply attach a clock face and hands to the quartz movement and you have a timepiece which will keep accurate time for a year and a half on one small battery. The body of the clock can be made from almost any material and in any shape that you desire. The joy of this book is that you can choose the style of clock you make to fit in with your particular craft skills, be they knitting, papier-mâché, salt dough, cross stitch or woodwork.

THE BODY OF THE CLOCK

The clock is made up of the following components: the movement, the spindle, the hands, dial and numerals. Numerals are not always necessary and can be left off completely or replaced with symbols, letters or pictures. There is a wonderful clock on a church in Dartmoor in Devon, which, instead of numerals, has letters spelling out MY DEAR MOTHER.

THE MOVEMENT

Quartz movements are measured in millimetres (or inches in the US). They come in a variety of sizes, so that the bigger the movement the longer and heavier the hands may be. They appear to work which ever way up they are put and are not too sensitive to damp and heat so they may be used in a kitchen or bathroom.

THE SPINDLE

The spindle, or shaft, is the part of the clock which sticks out of the middle of the movement, and passes from the back to the face of the clock. The hands are fitted on the spindle. The length of the spindle is important if the clock is to fit together properly so remember to work out the thickness of the clock before ordering the length of the spindle.

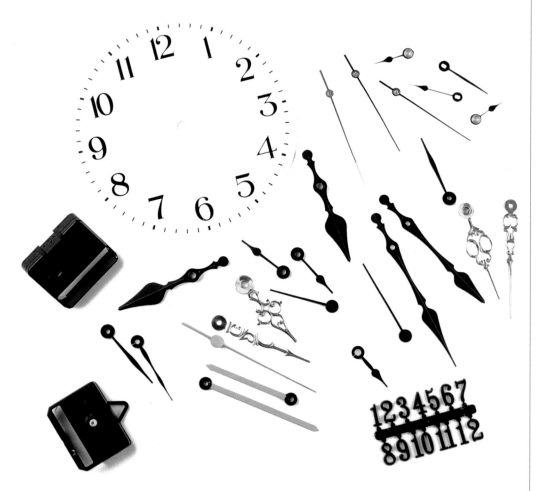

HANDS

These come in many shapes and sizes; they may be made of plastic or metal, or can be ornate or plain. Customize them by painting with enamel paint.

THE DIAL

You do not necessarily have to have a dial on a clock and as you will see from this book, many clocks do not have dials. To mark the four points on a dial simply make a cross and then mark the four points of 12, 9, 6, and 3. You can of course buy ready-printed dials which may be decorated or left plain.

NUMERALS

Numerals usually come in Roman or Arabic typefaces, but they can also be formed from dots or any motif you like. Buy them as individual self-adhesive numbers, as discs or on a dial.

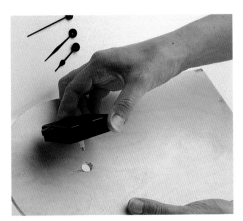

FITTING THE HANDS AND THE MOVEMENT

Most quartz clocks and fittings are similar to each other, and are very easy to fit. Drill a 10 mm (³⁄₈ in) hole in the clock and put the movement on the back; screw the fixing nut (most clocks will come with a fixing nut) into the movement from the front. Then carefully push the hands onto the end of the spindle taking care you don't bend the hands. Put in the battery and test to ensure that the hands will move freely.

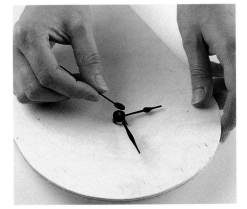

CHOOSING THE MOVEMENT

As a rough guide, short spindles fit up to a 4 mm (¹⁄₈ in) thickness, medium up to 10 mm (³⁄₈ in) and anything thicker needs a long spindle. For accuracy it is advisable to take a sample of your face materials with you when you buy the spindle. For grandfather-style clocks, a pendulum movement with a rod and bob is required.

SCULPTURAL CLOCKS

A wonderful collection of sculptural clocks, created from
a range of materials – glass, clay, wood, ceramics and salt
dough – perfectly illustrating that a clock can be any
shape you care to make it.

SCULPTURAL CLOCKS GALLERY

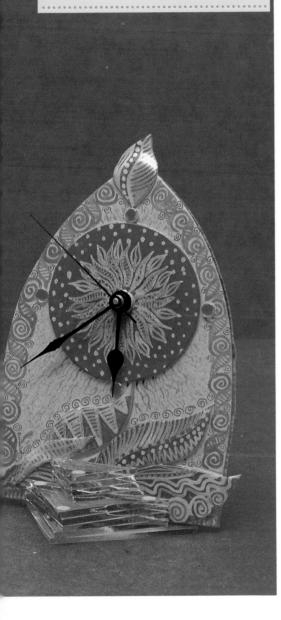

*G*lass Altars. Ann Wood's innovative glass designs are noted for their refreshing approach to pattern, colour and form. Created from traditional hot-glass techniques, much of her inspiration is drawn from ancient civilisations such as Egypt. *Ann Wood*

▲*T*wo precise time pieces for the mantelpiece. These clocks are made from PVC and laminates, which are printed by the clock maker before being cut into shapes and joined together. *Anne Finlay*

▶*G*lass Altar Design. The triangles placed one upon another make an altar with prisms of light. The triangle shape is used to create a random pattern on the blue glass. *Ann Wood*

▼*S*culptural clocks made from PVC and laminates, the designer uses other modern materials to create her very modern clocks; nylon, rubber and stainless steel. Note the tiny, brightly-coloured geometric shapes used instead of conventional hands. *Anne Finlay*

*E*nchanted or Magic Eye Clock. Made from synthetic self-hardening clay into which has been embedded curled wire strips. The clock is decorated using acrylic paints in the rich colours of the Middle East.
Ofer Acoo

*W*ild West clock made from salt dough. Cowboy boots, cacti and silver stars combine to create this themed wall clock. Studs are inserted before the dough is baked. *Cheryl Owen*

▼ *M*iniature Grandfather or Long Case Clock, small enough for a doll's house. The clock works on an old-fashioned spring mechanism. The decoration and colours are typical Eastern European folk art. *Author's collection*

▼ *A* David Mitchell glass clock, decorated with a symmetrical pattern in yellows, orange and blue. In the centre of the clock lurks a stylized insect. *David Mitchell*

▲ *M*odel of the clock tower in Clock Tower Mews, Islington, London. The clock face hides a secret compartment to store treasures. It is constructed from Balsa wood. Original Tower by Moxley and Frankl architects, model clock by *Tim Bertram.*

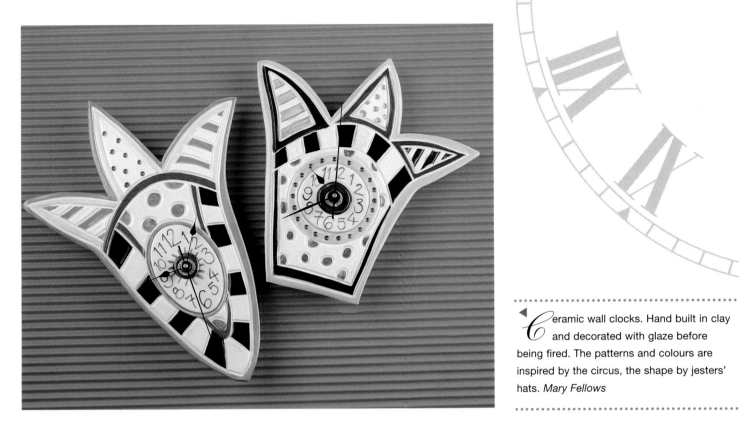

*C*eramic wall clocks. Hand built in clay and decorated with glaze before being fired. The patterns and colours are inspired by the circus, the shape by jesters' hats. *Mary Fellows*

*C*eramic mantle clock. What could be a rather traditional shape has an exuberance in its design captured by the bumps on its curved side and the decorative top knot or crown. The bright colours add to its general air of festivity. *Mary Fellows*

CLAY HEART CLOCK

*S*elf-hardening clay is clay which does not need to be fired to become hard. It is a good material for clock making but allow at least a day for drying out before beginning to decorate. When moulding the clay make sure you keep your hands moist as this will make handling the clay a lot easier.

1 Roll out a piece of clay and cut out a heart shape with a knife. Make a hole in the centre for the clock spindle to pass through.

2 Attach small balls of clay round the edge of the heart and make a small hole in each using a sharp modelling tool or a skewer.

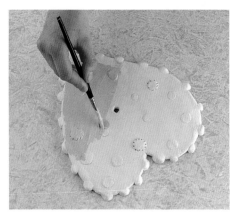

3 Mould four spots of clay onto the face of the clock for the numerals and pierce small holes around each spot.

4 Leave the clock to dry for several days until it is hard. Then paint it, first applying a mauve base coat.

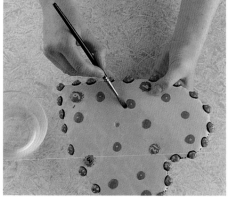

5 Colour the spots in purple and pink and paint in the numerals in blue and yellow. When the paint is dry, apply a coat of clear polyurethane varnish. Leave to dry and then attach the clock movement and hands.

GOTHIC CLOCK

*T*his clock involves making a latex mould which allows multiple use so that several matching clocks can be produced. If you only want to make one clock just form the master from self-hardening clay.

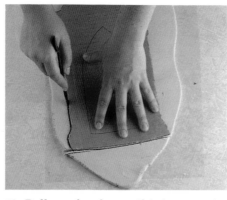

1 Roll out the clay until it is approximately 2.5 cm (1 in) deep. Scale up the template provided to the size required, transfer to thick card and cut out. Place the template on top of the clay and cut out the design.

2 Mould the shapes in relief using modelling tools and leave to dry. This will take about 6 days. Paint the model with 20 coats of rubber latex solution leaving the latex to dry between coats.

4 When the plaster sets, remove the clay wall and release the master rubber latex mould. Wash the mould with water. Put the master aside and place the rubber mould in the plaster shell you have just made. Mix more plaster and pour it into the rubber mould.

5 Embed a metal hook in the back as the plaster begins to harden so that the clock may be hung on the wall later. Leave the plaster for half an hour to set and then release from the mould, pulling up on the metal hook. Sand the edges smooth.

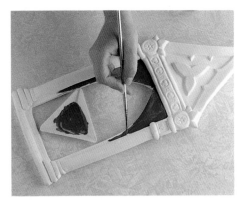

3 Leave the latex on top of the model and build a clay wall round it which is higher than the model. Mix the plaster of Paris according to the manufacturer's instructions and pour it over the master latex mould.

6 Paint with acrylic paints. Cut a piece of plywood to fit in the back of the clock and paint with acrylic paints. Glue the plywood to the back of the clock using strong, clear glue. Make a hole for the spindle and fit the clock movement and hands.

SALT DOUGH TEAPOT CLOCK

YOU WILL NEED

small plate
silver foil
325 g/8 oz/ 2¾ cups flour
325 g/8 oz/2¾ cups salt
2 tbsps vegetable oil
200 ml/7 fl oz/¾ cup water
rolling pin
trefoil (shamrock)-shaped aspic cutter
skewer
baking tray
baking parchment (parchment paper)
florist's wire
scissors
cream and blue acrylic paints
paintbrushes
clear acrylic varnish
clock movement and hands

*S*alt dough is easy to prepare and is so versatile almost any shape can be sculpted from it.

1 Turn the plate over and cover the underside with silver foil, padding out the centre if necessary so that it is slightly raised.

2 Mix together the flour, salt, vegetable oil and water to form the dough. Knead thoroughly and roll out a circle slightly larger than the plate. Lay over the foil, cut a circle in the centre for the spindle and trim to size.

3 Roll sausage shapes for the lid, trim and base. Dampen both dough surfaces before positioning the pieces and press them firmly into place.

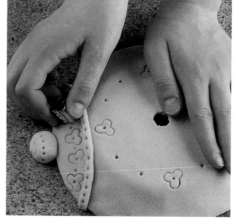

4 Shape and add the spout. Mark the flower design using a trefoil (shamrock)-shaped aspic cutter and the end of a skewer. Each flower represents a numeral. Prick a dot pattern along the lid and base.

5 Place on a baking tray covered with baking parchment (parchment paper). Bake for a minimum of 4 - 5 hours at 110°C/225°F/Gas ¼. After one hour, take out of the oven and allow to cool. Bend a short length of florist's wire into a handle shape and cover with dough. Fix to the body clock.

6 Return to the oven for about four hours. Allow to cool and carefully remove the plate. Paint the clock with cream acrylic paint and leave to dry. Paint the flowers pale blue and pick out the details in dark blue.

7 Cover with several coats of clear acrylic varnish, allowing the varnish to dry between coats. Fit the clock movements and hands.

JESTER CLOCK

*T*his pretty clock is made almost solely from clay with a little wire to hold the components together.

1 Make a big pinch pot from the clay, making sure it is large enough to take the clock movement, and flatten the front and the base.

2 Mark a circle on the front of the pot, using a pair of compasses. Enlarge the central hole until the clock spindle will pass through.

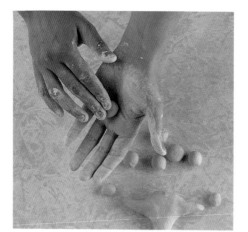

3 Mould a jester's hat shape and 6 small clay balls.

4 Score patterns onto the clock face and balls using a modelling tool. Using wire cutters, cut 3 short lengths of wire. Stick these into the three points on the hat shape. Stick a small ball of clay on the end of each wire.

5 Stick all the components together using wood glue. Place the jester's hat on top of the pinch pot and 3 balls down each side.

6 Leave to dry out thoroughly. This may take a couple of days. Decorate the clock using acrylic paints. When dry, coat with clear acrylic varnish and leave to dry once again. Fit the clock movement and hands.

MOSAIC CLOCK

*T*his pretty clock looks like a miniature patchwork quilt. Calculate the size of the plywood so that you can fit in an even number of tiles, without having to use any extra broken pieces.

YOU WILL NEED
rectangle of thin plywood
sandpaper
ready-mixed tile grout
grout spreader
assorted mosaic tiles
4 black textured mosaic tiles
strong, clear glue
drill
clock movement and hands

1 Sand the edges of the plywood until smooth and wipe with a damp cloth.

2 Spread a generous layer of ready-mixed grout onto the plywood until it is evenly covered.

3 Drill a hole in the centre and cover the grout with mosaic tiles, choosing the colours as you go. Leave a space around the hole and paint blue.

4 When the surface has been completely covered with tiles, stick on black textured mosaic tiles to act as numerals using strong, clear glue. When the grout has dried, attach the clock movement and hands.

11 12 1

STRAWBERRY SALT DOUGH CLOCK

his tartan-effect clock is durable, being made from salt dough.
The fruit motifs provide a focal point for the numerals.

YOU WILL NEED
325 g/11 oz/ 2¾ cups plain flour,
plus extra for dusting
325 g/11 oz/ 2¾ cups salt
200 ml/7 fl oz/ ¾ cup water
2 tbsp vegetable oil
airtight container
rolling pin
kitchen knife
baking sheet
baking parchment (parchment
paper)
ready-made gesso
paintbrushes
acrylic paints in red, blue, green
and pink
clear acrylic varnish

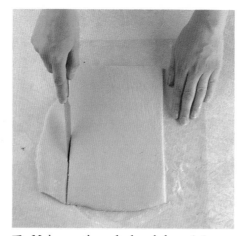

1 Make up the salt dough by mixing together the flour, salt, water and oil. Knead well and leave to rest in an airtight container for approximately half an hour. Roll out the dough to a thickness of approximately 2.5 cm (1 in) on a surface dusted with flour. Cut out a rectangle using a kitchen knife.

2 Mould 7 strawberry shapes (3 large, 4 small) and prick 'pip' markings with the point of the knife. Attach the large strawberries to the top of the rectangle, and the smaller ones in the place of the numbers 3, 6, 9 and 12. If necessary, dab with water to help them stick. Bake in the oven on a baking tray covered with baking parchment (parchment paper) for approximately 8 hours at 110°C/225°F/Gas ¼ or until it hardens.

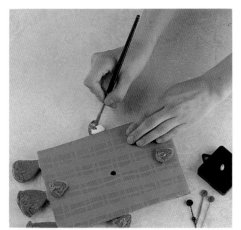

3 When the clock has hardened, remove from the oven and leave to cool for half an hour. Drill a hole in the centre. Decorate the hands of the clock with dots of paint and leave to dry. Paint on a coat of ready-made gesso and leave to dry before painting the clock face and the strawberries. When dry, apply a coat of clear acrylic varnish and leave to dry once again.

4 Fit the clock movement and hands to complete the piece.

BROKEN CHINA CLOCK

*C*ollecting broken china is easy, and here it is put to good use.
Keep an eye out for special pieces when digging in the garden
or walking by a river or on a beach.

1 Using a drill, make a hole in the centre of the box to take the spindle. Colour the grout by adding a small amount of purple acrylic paint. Mix well using an old fork.

2 Cover the outside of the box with grout using the grout spreader. Arrange the pieces of china and sink them into the grout. Remember to avoid covering the central hole.

3 Repeat along the sides of the box, choosing smaller pieces of china.

4 Fill in any gaps with grout, wiping off any excess with a cloth rag. Leave the grout to dry and then attach the clock movement and hands.

PAINT & GILT CLOCKS

A colourful selection of painted and gilded clocks to captivate and inspire. Whether you are decorating enamel, papier-mâché or wood, painting is a simple yet effective way of transforming an ordinary clock face into something highly individual.

PAINT AND GILT CLOCKS GALLERY

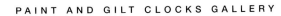

*T*hese beautiful clocks are made of ceramic onto which is applied layers of papier-mâché before being painted in rich turquoise or plum and highlighted in gold.
Jenni Robson, Tic Toc Designs

*T*he ever popular star theme is put to good use in these three clocks. The large clock on the left is made from wood and is by *Kate Lang*. The two smaller clocks with stars are by *Sally Bourne*.

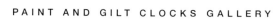

*R*osie Casseldon decorates clocks to look feminine and country-like in tone. She hand-paints three-dimensional flowers and forms from nature onto natural wood or MDF. *Rosie Casseldon, tictoc*

*S*un clock domed in the centre. Constructed from papier-mâché worked over a ceramic base. The raised centre allows the hands to pass over the raised sun image on the right-hand side. *Jenni Robson, Tic Toc Designs*

A sporting clock for the keen golfer. A great idea for a birthday present is to paint the hobby of your nearest and dearest onto a clock. *Rosie Casseldon, tictoc*

*P*apier-mâché clocks which appear to look like rich leather or fabric. The edge of the clock on the right is made by using a glue gun and then painted gold. *Jenni Robson, Tic Toc Designs*

*R*ed poppies on a pure white background. This clock needs no numerals or other decoration. A clock for a country kitchen or living room. *Rosie Casseldon, tictoc*

*A*n old enamel plate has been decorated with fruits and vegetables to make a superb kitchen clock. *Loaned by Mr and Mrs Frankl-Bertram*

◀ *T*hree ceramic wall clocks by Isobel Dennis. Isobel makes her own moulds for the basic shapes and for the flowers and leaves which are made in relief and stuck onto the basic shape before firing. The clocks are hand glazed after a biscuit fire, before finally firing to fix the glaze.

Isobel Dennis

MARINER'S COMPASS CLOCK

*T*his clock has a nautical theme, inspired by the traditional designs of seafarers' mementoes, and uses recycled floor boarding as its base.

1 Using the template provided as a guide, drill a hole the same size as the clock spindle. Sand the edges of the wood until smooth. Paint with wood primer and leave to dry.

2 Scale up and trace the design from the template. Transfer onto the primed wood by marking through the tracing paper onto the wood below using prick marks made by the point of a pair of compasses as guides to the position of the design.

3 Join the prick marks by drawing straight lines in pencil.

4 Paint the compass black and white and the background blue.

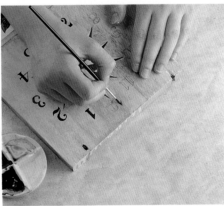

5 Paint the numerals round the compass points using black acrylic paint and a fine brush.

6 Paint in the yellow band and the floral design.

7 Cut the moulding using a mitre saw to fit the edges of the clock baseboard. Paint the frame black and fix on with wood glue. Make sure the corners are flush. When the paint is dry, fit the clock movement and hands.

SUN AND MOON CLOCK

thin plywood
drill
red matt emulsion (flat latex) paint
paintbrushes
tracing paper
chalk
pencil
Japanese gold size
sheets of gold and silver Dutch
metal leaf
pine-coloured antique varnish
clock movement and hands

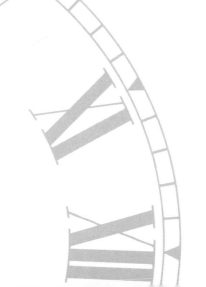

*G*old and silver foils combine in a simple, yet effective, way to add glamour and magic to this clock.

1 Cut a circle of wood to the size you require your clock to be and drill a hole in the centre for the spindle. Paint with 2 coats of red matt emulsion (flat latex) paint, allowing to dry between coats.

2 Using the template provided, trace the design onto tracing paper. Rub plenty of chalk onto the back of the paper.

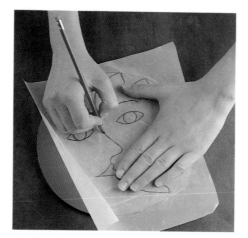

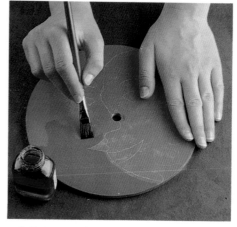

3 Lay the tracing paper, chalk side down on the wooden circle, and firmly draw over with a pencil to transfer the design onto the wood.

4 Paint on the Japanese gold size leaving the chalk lines showing. Leave until it is almost dry to the touch. Do one side first and then the other to achieve a clear central line.

5 Place the Dutch gold leaf over the tacky size and press down with your hand. Remove the transfer paper from the back of the gold leaf. Repeat with the second part of the design using the silver leaf.

6 Wipe off the chalk lines and then apply pine-coloured antique varnish to fix and give a distressed look. Add the clock movement and hands.

CAT CLOCK

YOU WILL NEED

white paper
pencil
scissors
thick white card
craft knife
acrylic paints in orange, pink, black
and green
paintbrushes
clear acrylic varnish
numerals
strong, clear glue
clock movement and hands

*T*his clock is similar to old-fashioned dummy boards which were once popular. The cat pattern can be enlarged to the size you prefer.

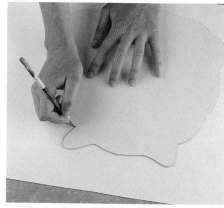

1 Scale up the cat template to the size required and transfer it to white paper. Cut out using scissors.

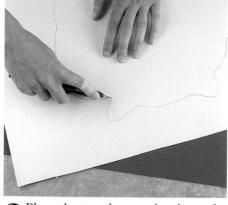

2 Place the template on the sheet of thick white card and draw round it in pencil.

4 Draw in the cat's features in pencil. Paint the cat's fur using orange acrylic paint.

5 Paint the inside of the ears pink, the eyes green, and add whiskers and outline the eyes and ears in black. When dry, apply a coat of clear acrylic varnish and leave to dry. Stick on the numerals around the clock face (as if floating in a saucer of milk), using clear, strong glue. Fit the clock movement and hands.

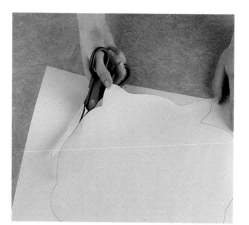

3 Mark the place for the clock spindle. Cut out the cat shape using a craft knife.

HEART AND RIBBONS CLOCK

YOU WILL NEED
white paper
pencil
scissors
thick white card
craft knife
acrylic paints in red, yellow, pink
and white
paintbrushes
clear acrylic varnish
clock movement and hands

*T*his clock will make a great Valentine present. You could even inscribe the name of the one you love.

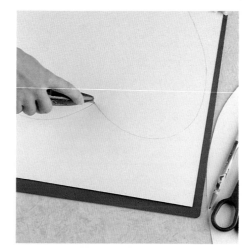

1 Draw a heart template on white paper. Draw round it in pencil onto the thick white card and cut out using a craft knife.

2 Paint the heart shape using red acrylic paints and leave to dry. Drill a hole in the centre for the spindle.

3 Draw in the outlines of the ribbons with a pencil.

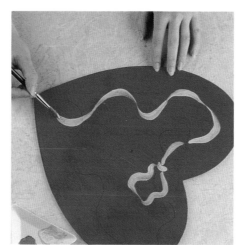

4 Paint the base colour for the ribbons, yellow on one side and pink on the other.

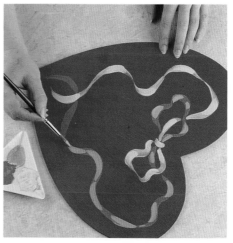

5 Add some white paint to mix paler pink and yellow shades. Paint in the highlights on the ribbons and leave to dry. Apply a coat of clear acrylic varnish and fit the clock movement and hands.

JEWELLED NUMBER CLOCKS

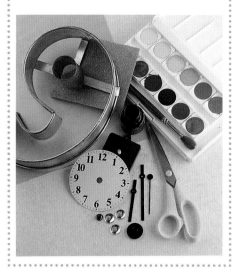

*T*hese clock designs are made from a very thin plywood which can be cut using scissors, making it suitable for use in children's projects.

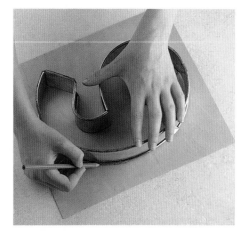

1 Scale up the template provided to the size you require, or use a number cake tin (pan). Draw around it onto a piece of paper and cut out. Place on the plywood and draw round it.

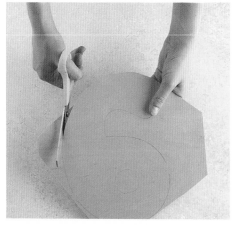

2 Cut out the shape using scissors. When cutting plywood, cut into the corners and then cut out from them rather than following the contours as if cutting out paper. This also helps prevent the plywood from splitting.

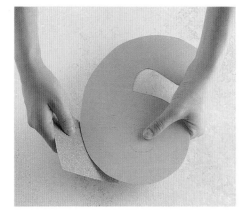

3 Sand the edges with sandpaper until they are smooth.

4 Using acrylic paint, apply the blue base colour to the front of the number and leave to dry.

5 Pour a small amount of glass paint into a saucer. Gently apply it to the clock face and leave to dry (approximately 24 hours). It is important to work in a dust-free environment.

6 Mark the point for the clock fitting and then pierce with an awl. Once a small hole has been made, insert a sharp pencil to make a larger hole.

7 Stick the jewels onto the clock using PVA glue. Stick on the clock face and add the sun-ray decoration using gold craft paint. Fit the clock movement and hands.

YOU WILL NEED
2 pieces of thin plywood, each 14.5 x 18 cm (5¾ x 7 in)
pine block, 14.5 x 18 cm (5¾ x 7 in), 3 cm (1¼ in) deep
pair of compasses
masking tape
sandpaper
fretsaw (scroll saw)
drill
wood glue
paintbrushes
small piece of 3 mm (⅛ in) plywood
pencil
paper
white matt emulsion (flat latex) paint
acrylic paints in cream, blue, green, yellow, red and white
gold craft paint
clear polyurethane varnish
screw-in pendulum clock movements and hands
brass screw
screwdriver

DANDELION CLOCK

The pendulum clock mechanism is set inside this clock, and is accessible through a little door at the back.

1 Place a piece of plywood on top of the pine block and draw a curve at one end using a pair of compasses.

2 Join the pieces of wood using masking tape to hold them steady. Cut along the curve using a fretsaw (scroll saw). Sand the edges smooth.

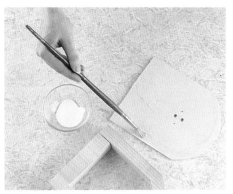

4 Remembering that the dial must be placed high enough up to leave space for the clock movement and pendulum, drill 2 small and 2 large holes through the front piece of plywood. The smaller holes are for the fixing screws, and the larger ones for the clock spindle and the winding key. Stick the front panel to the block using wood glue.

5 Scale up the templates provided to the size required to fit on the front of the clock. Transfer the templates to the thin plywood and cut out. Sand the edges smooth.

3 Remove the plywood and use the fretsaw (scroll saw) to cut out the middle of the pine block. Place the second piece of plywood over the hole and draw a curve slightly larger than the hole. This piece forms the back door. Cut out the curve.

6 Prime all the pieces of the clock and its decorations using white matt emulsion (flat latex) paint. Stipple the clock case using a top coat of cream acrylic paint.

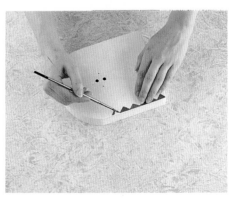

7 Using acrylic paint, add blue triangles around the front edges of the clock, and paint on a clock face in blue with white details. Colour the leaves and dandelion flower using acrylic paints, and edge them with gold craft paint. When dry, apply a coat of clear polyurethane varnish to all the clock pieces, and leave to dry again.

8 Fix the clock movement and hands inside the clock. Stick the dandelion and leaves to the front of the clock using wood glue. Paint a dandelion motif on the back door and position the plywood over the pine block. Drill a hole through the plywood and into the pine to hold the brass screw for the back door. Screw in place.

PAPER CLOCKS

Working with paper is fun and easy to do. Using papier-mâché
and découpage techniques, the projects in this section will
provide an idea of how versatile paper is and illustrate the
exciting and innovative clocks that can be made with
the simplest of materials.

PAPER CLOCKS GALLERY

◀ *C*artoon cat clock made from papier-mâché and edged in self-hardening clay. The purple, turquoise and yellow colours suit the silly grin on the cat's face. *Amanda Blunden*

▶ *C*arriage clocks made from hand-made paper which have been made from pulp and then dyed. The collage effect is achieved by ripping and layering paper onto a basic card shape. *Gerry Copp*

▶ *O*ne distorted face made from paper, almost Alice in Wonderland like in its appeal. Two purely abstract designs using the same colours as the face and similar marks to show it is the work of the same designer. *Pampas Design*

◄ *A* surreal découpaged clock of an angelic Italian face with fish floating by, above and below. The powerful image is enhanced by the use of just black and white. *Josephine Whitfield*

► *A* very pretty clock made from the simplest materials. Constructed from one small frilled doilly on a flat paper doilly stuck onto a cardboard base. Hang up with wide white satin ribbon. *Josephine Whitfield*

▼ *A* collection of découpaged carriage and mantle clocks all evoking feelings of nostalgia. *Roger Lascelles Clocks Ltd*

◀ *G*old leaf surrounds an astrological map taken from the cover of a book and découpaged onto plywood. The rich image belies the humble materials used.
Emma Whitfield

▶ *M*antle clock made from card covered in papier-mâché and decorated with builder's filler (spackle) to add a three-dimensional aspect to the surface decoration. Colours are painted one upon another and then scratched through with a blunt instrument to reveal the layers beneath. The eyes and gold decoration reveal an Indian influence. *Katherine Reekie*

▶ *A* funny Victorian lady découpaged with a clock on her stomach. The clock was taken from a magazine and then enlarged on a colour photocopier before being cut out and stuck in position.
Josephine Whitfield

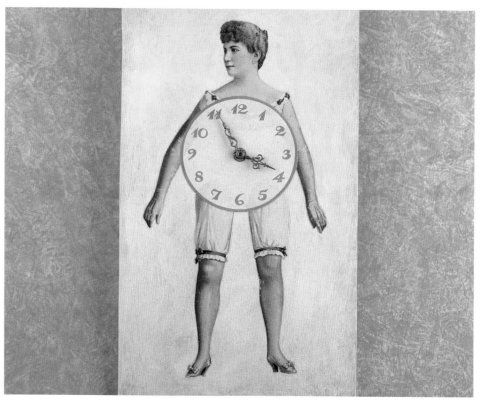

PAPIER-MÂCHÉ GRANDFATHER CLOCK

The versatile yet tough nature of papier-mâché makes it ideal for this large, free-standing clock.

YOU WILL NEED

large sheets of cardboard
pencil
craft knife
masking tape
flexible corrugated card
wallpaper paste
water
old newspaper
thin plywood for clock face
coping saw
hand drill
white matt emulsion (flat latex) paint
paintbrushes
sandpaper
assorted poster paints
clear polyurethane varnish
pendulum clock movement with rod
and bob, and hands

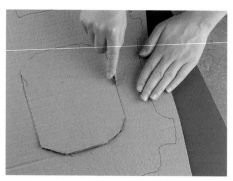

1 Scale up the templates provided to the size required and transfer to the sheets of cardboard. Cut out the pieces with a craft knife.

2 Fix the side pieces of card with masking tape to the front sections to form the wall between the front and back pieces of the clock.

4 For the papier-mâché, prepare the wallpaper paste by mixing it with water according to the manufacturer's instructions. Tear or cut strips of newspaper about 5 cm (2 in) wide and dip them into the paste. Cover the clock with strips of papier-mâché. Draw a circle of thin plywood for the clock face; this should be slightly smaller than the front area it will sit on. Cut out with a coping saw and cover with a layer of papier-mâché strips. When dry, drill a hole in the centre to take the spindle. Place the clock face to the front of the case, fixing it in place with more papier-mâché strips. Continue covering the whole clock in papier-mâché until you have laid down a total of 5 layers.

3 Put extra pieces of cardboard across the inside of the middle of the clock to strengthen it. Using masking tape, add corrugated card to the front and side to shape the sides.

5 Prime the clock with 2 coats of white matt emulsion (flat latex) paint, leaving the paint to dry between coats.

6 Form decorative details and numerals from papier-mâché and position them on the clock. When dry, sand smooth and then apply another coat of white matt emulsion (flat latex) paint. Paint the clock and the decorative details using poster paints. Two coats of paint may be necessary in parts for an even layer of colour. When dry, add a layer of clear polyurethane varnish.

7 Cut out 2 cardboard heart shapes and tape them over the bob of the pendulum with masking tape. Apply strips of papier-mâché over the bob and leave to dry. Prime with white matt emulsion (flat latex) paint and colour with poster paint. Varnish. When dry, fit the clock movement, pendulum and hands into the case.

MANTEL CLOCK

*T*hese papier-mâché clocks represent the juxtaposition of a traditional clock shape with a contemporary style of decoration. The instructions are to make the clock on the left.

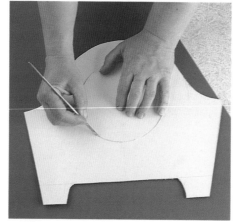

1 Scale up the templates provided to the size required and transfer to thick card. Cut out with a scalpel.

2 Construct the clock body by sticking panels together with strips of gummed tape.

3 Tear newspaper into strips. Mix the wallpaper paste with water according to the manufacturer's instructions. Dip each strip into the paste and smooth over the card. Continue until the card is completely covered. Apply three layers in all, allowing each layer to dry before applying the next.

4 When the papier-mâché is dry, coat with white matt emulsion (flat latex) paint. This seals the papier-mâché and gives a smooth surface on which to paint.

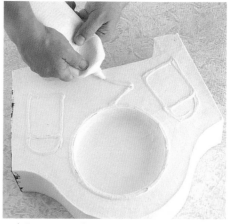

5 Decorate the case with plaster filler squeezed straight from the tube and leave to dry.

11

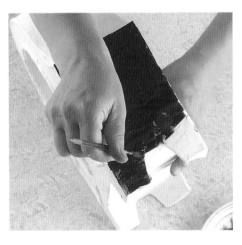

6 Paint with blue acrylic paint and
scratch squiggly patterns through
the paint using the end of the paintbrush. Stick on the plastic jewels using
PVA glue. Cut rectangles from an old
postcard to fit in the front panels and
glue on. Cut numerals out of spare
paper and paint gold. Colour the raised
decorative details with gold craft paint,
and paint the clock face silver. When
dry, stick down the numerals. Apply a
coat of clear polyurethane varnish and
leave to dry. Make a hole for the spindle using a pair of scissors, and fit the
clock movement and hands.

TRIPLE-FACED CLOCK

This unusual clock has three faces but only one tells
the time!

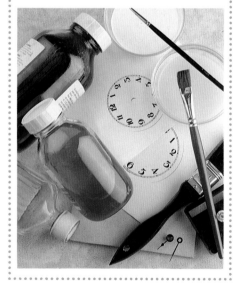

1 Sand the plywood and prime with 2 coats of white matt emulsion (flat latex) paint. Drill a hole in the centre.

2 Cut out the photocopies of the clock faces with scissors. Stick them down one above the other on the plywood, making sure the centre of the middle one sits over the spindle hole.

3 Paint clock hands on the top and bottom faces using black acrylic paint. Paint a line round the edge of the clock in black oil paint.

4 Paint on a coat of clear acrylic varnish to seal the paper. Leave to dry.

5 Paint on a coat of antique varnish and wait until dry to the touch (usually about an hour, depending on humidity). Paint on the crackle varnish and wait for the cracks to appear.

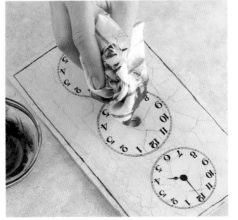

6 When the cracks appear, mix raw umber oil paint with a little turpentine and immediately rub it into the cracks using a soft rag.

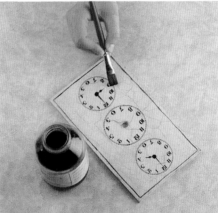

7 Paint on a final coat of antique varnish. Leave to dry. Fit the clock mechanism and hands.

SUNSET CLOCK

This lively clock uses the traditional sun motif in a new way, setting it between wooden shutters in a window.

1 Turn the dark blue card over so as not to mark the coloured side. Using a pencil, draw along a ruler to measure out a rectangle for the base board. Cut out the rectangle using scissors.

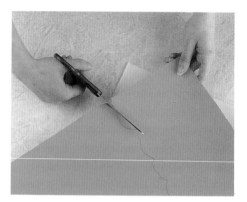

2 Draw a wavy cloud outline in pencil on the green card. Make sure that the width of the cloud is wide enough to pass under the area where the shutters will be placed. Cut along the wavy outline using scissors. Repeat with the paler blue card.

3 Cut two tall rectangles from the white card, making sure they are the same height as the base board of the clock. Using the template provided, cut out 9 sun rays from the gold paper. Draw a circle on the gold paper using the compasses, and cut out.

4 Stick down the sun's face in the centre of the blue base board. Glue the green cloud outline so that it slightly overlaps the base of the sun's face, and then add the pale blue cloud flush with the base of the board, but overlapping the bottom of the green cloud. Arrange and glue down the sun's rays and stick on the white shutter pieces.

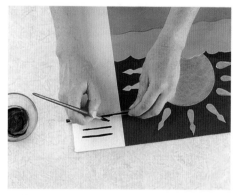

5 Resting the paintbrush against a pen or other straight edge, paint in the slats of the shutters using black poster paint. Leave to dry and then apply a coat of oak-coloured matt (flat) acrylic varnish. This will protect the clock as well as giving it an antique look. When dry, fit the clock movement and hands in the centre of the sun.

DÉCOUPAGE FLOWER CLOCK

A pretty clock in the shape of a flower made from simple,
yet effective materials.

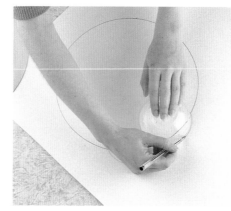

1 Draw round a large plate onto white card, leaving enough space around the plate to make cup-sized petals. Draw round a cup or small bowl to make semi-circular petals all the way round the rim of the large circle.

2 Using a craft knife, cut out the flower shape from card and pierce the centre with an awl to make the hole for the spindle.

3 Use the flower shape as a template to draw onto the back of the gold paper. Cut out the gold paper flower with scissors.

4 Cut out flowers and leaves from the wrapping paper or magazine cuttings. Stick the gold flower onto the card base using PVA glue.

5 Arrange the flowers and leaves on the gold background and stick down using PVA glue. Wipe off any excess glue using a damp cloth.

6 Apply a coat of clear acrylic varnish, and leave to dry. Fit the clock movement and hands.

NATURAL CLOCKS

A lively mixture of natural and organic materials – wood, string, slate, metal and dried flowers – are featured in the clocks in this section. These flexible materials can all be re-cycled and offer the opportunity to create wonderful and unusual clocks for minimum outlay.

NATURAL CLOCKS GALLERY

*T*he two clocks on the left are by Bruce Jacobs. Cleverly balanced on a coil of metal formed to look like a spring, the clock on the far left is reaching for the stars whilst the one in the middle is more earth bound. The clock on the right is made by Adject design. A diamond shape is supported on rather spindly legs. *Bruce Jacobs/Adject Design*

*M*aura Heslop has successfully turned her jewellery technique of iodizing aluminium into a way of producing very imaginative and interesting clocks. The one on the left is a combination of wild and wacky birds, the one on the right a more simple-shaped vehicle suitable for a child's room. *Maura Heslop*

*L*ouise Slater uses found objects, i.e. pebbles in a very modern way. The pebbles are tumbled so they are smooth. Carefully chosen for weight and size, they are attached to a laminate background using nylon coated wire. *Louise Slater*

*A*n attractive steel sun is scorched to give an interesting surface before the clock mechanism is fitted.

Richard Pell

*P*atented by time. This artist has produced a range of cut-out metal clocks finished in verdigris and rust shades. Although it has an air of antiquity the maker's approach is distinctly modern.

Ryan Soloman

*S*late, drift wood, nuts and bolts and all other forms of flotsam and jetsam from our wasteful industrial age go into forming these modern clocks. *Chris Conroy*

*T*his impressive arched clock is exquisitely decorated with intricate inlay work featuring a detailed pattern of tiny symbols. As for many artists, the clock forms a versatile showcase for individual expression and artistic skill. *Tania Schwartz*

*C*onstructed from separate metallic pieces and then assembled together, these clocks are restrained and modernist in design. They include the option of humorous metallic antennae. *Adrian Thompson*

SPIDER'S WEB CLOCK

*T*he motto inscribed on the slate base board is an old Latin favourite: "tempus fugit" or "time flies". Slate tiles can often be found in local skips, or ask builders if they have an odd tile lying around.

YOU WILL NEED
slate roofing tile
drill
tracing paper
pencil
white wax crayon
pair of compasses or engraving tool
lino-cutting tools
1.5 m (60 in) 4.5 cm (1¾ in) wooden moulding
fretsaw (scroll saw)
wood glue
bronze and silver acrylic paints
paintbrushes
hot glue gun
clock movement and hands

1 Carefully drill a hole in the centre of the slate the same size as the clock spindle. Scale up and trace the two templates provided and transfer them to the slate by rubbing white wax crayon on the back of the traced design. Put the crayon side against the tile, and trace with a pencil.

2 Using a sharp implement such as the point from a pair of compasses or engraving tool, mark the spokes of the web and then draw in the lines between the spokes.

3 Draw in the letters using the sharp tool.

4 Trace the border design and transfer to the slate in 2 halves.

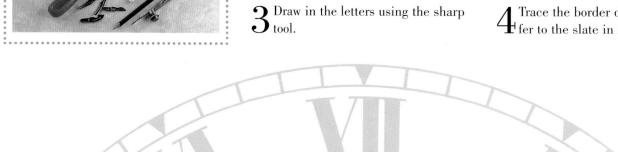

5 Use the lino-cutting tools to engrave the border patterns onto the tile.

6 Using a fretsaw (scroll saw) cut the wooden moulding to form a frame for the slate making sure corners are square. Stick the frame together using wood glue. Leave to dry. Paint with bronze acrylic paint and highlight the moulding in silver acrylic paint.

7 Attach the frame to the slate using a hot glue gun. Add the clock movement and hands.

STRING CLOCK

*S*ave your odd pieces of string and rope to put together this inventive clock.

1 Cut out a rectangle of cardboard measuring 24 x 30 cm (9½ x 12 in) with a craft knife and ruler.

2 Glue the clock face in the centre of the cardboard positioned towards the top edge. Using a sharp pencil, pierce a hole in the cardboard for the clock spindle.

4 Secure the ends of the rope by wrapping with strong thread and then stitching it in place.

5 To make the tassels, cut a piece of string approximately 20 cm (8 in) in length and with one end form 3 loops. Twist the other end tightly around the base of the loops and secure with strong thread. Cut the bottom of the long loops and fray.

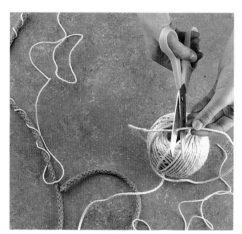

3 Twist string round the rope and secure the ends with a needle and thread. Cut lengths of string and wrap them around the longest piece of rope.

6 Paint small areas of the cardboard with PVA glue. Add lengths of string in coils and trails around the clock face, pressing down to fix in place. When dry, add the clock movement and hands.

WOODLAND CLOCK

*T*his pretty dried flower arrangement conceals the unexpected
face of a clock.

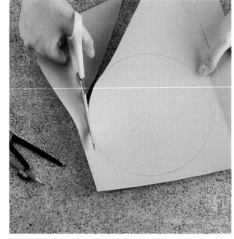

1 Using a pair of compasses, draw a
circle on thin card to match the
diameter of the twig wreath. Cut out the
circle with scissors.

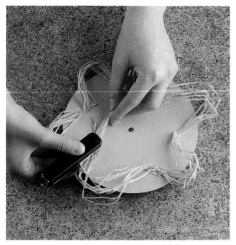

2 Make a hole in the centre of the
clock using an awl. Loop raffia
around the card circle and staple in
place.

3 Stick the clock face in the centre of
the card with PVA glue, making
sure the spindle holes in the face and
card are aligned. Glue raffia around the
edge of the clock face.

4 Position the twig wreath over the
clock face and stitch in place using
strong thread, passing through the card
and between some of the twigs.

5 Weave more raffia through the first set of raffia loops to cover the rest of the card showing.

6 Stick dried flower heads onto the twig wreath with small dabs of PVA glue. Add the clock movement and hands.

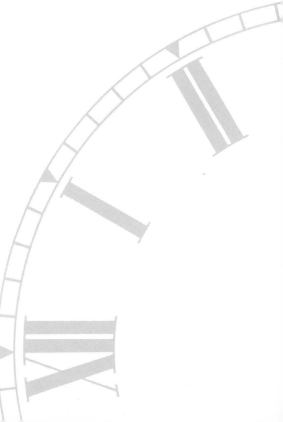

PRESSED FLOWER CLOCK

A piece of board cut into a traditional mantel clock decorated with pressed flowers, leaves and buds makes this a most unusual clock.

1 Scale up the clock outline from the template provided to the size required. Transfer to the plywood and cut out using a fretsaw (scroll saw). Sand the edges smooth.

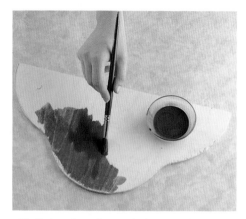

2 Paint the plywood shape using diluted green craft paint.

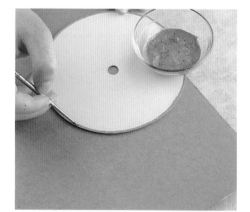

3 Using a pair of compasses, draw a 14 cm (5½ in) circle on the cream mounting board and cut out using a craft knife. Drill a hole in the centre of both the card and the wooden shape to take the spindle. Paint a thin line of gold ink around the circle edge.

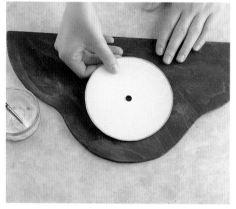

4 Glue the circle in the centre of the clock shape using PVA glue. Make sure the spindle holes align.

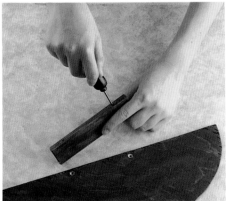

5 Drill 2 small holes in the base of the clock shape, and countersink the holes on the right side. Paint the soft wood stand green and, when dry, make corresponding holes in it.

6 Arrange the pressed flowers and leaves in your chosen pattern. Stick the flowers and leaves on the clock shape using latex adhesive. Add tiny buds for the numerals.

7 Screw on the soft wood stand. Cover the clock with several coats of clear polyurethane varnish, allowing to dry between coats. Fit the clock movement and hands.

OAK-LEAF CLOCK

The glittering oak leaves surrounding this clock are created from recycled metal and yet add an air of opulence. Be careful when cutting out the oak leaves as the edges of the tomato paste tubes can be quite sharp.

YOU WILL NEED

soft rag
red glass paint
clock face
paper
pencil
scissors
tomato paste tubes, cut in half when finished, and cleaned
piece of card
strong, clear glue
awl
clock movement and hands

1 Using a soft rag, apply the glass paint to the clock face and leave to dry for 24 hours in a dust-free area.

2 Scale up the leaf template provided to the size required and cut out using scissors. Place the tomato paste packet metal side down and draw round the template in pencil. Draw in the veins. Repeat until you have enough leaves to surround the clock.

3 Using scissors, cut out the leaf shapes. Cut a disc of card the same size as the dial and stick the leaves round the edge using strong, clear glue. Stick the dial on top of the card and then make a hole with an awl in the centre of the clock for the spindle. Fit the clock movement and the hands.

DRIFTWOOD CLOCK

*C*ollect pieces of sea-smoothed, sun-faded driftwood and with a little imagination they can be turned into a clock.

1 Cut out a rectangle from the plywood large enough to contain the pieces of driftwood. Find the centre of the plywood and drill a hole. Paint the board with blue acrylic paint and leave to dry.

2 Using wood glue, stick the driftwood round the edge of the board making a frame.

3 Attach the length of rope to the back of the clock using strong, clear glue.

4 Using strong, clear glue stick on the small starfish to form numerals for the clock face. Arrange and stick down the small shells on the driftwood.

5 Paint the clock hands and decorate with small dots of blue acrylic paint. When dry, fix the hands and the movement in place.

TOMATO CLOCK

This clock is decorated using motifs from recycled cans. Take great care when working with sharp edges and keep the components away from children.

YOU WILL NEED
rectangle of thin wood, 25 x 28 cm (10 x 11 in)
strong craft knife
drill
tomato paste cans, cleaned
metal (tin) snips or scissors
strong, clear glue
9 metal nuts
clock movement and hands

1 Drill a hole in the centre of the wood to take the spindle. Using a strong craft knife, make a fine slit along one side of the square, approximately 3 mm (⅛ in) deep.

2 Stick a row of 9 nuts along one side of the square, using strong, clear glue.

3 Cut out 4 crown shapes from the cans and add borders of metal (use a contrasting colour if possible), gluing in place. Also cut out the numbers 3, 6, 9 and 12. If there are any tomatoes printed on the can cut out 8. Alternatively cut out any 8 metal dots.

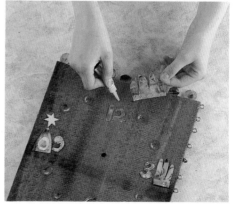

4 Glue the numerals in position around the clock face, add the crowns beside each numeral, and stick down the tomatoes or other metal dots in the place of the other numerals. Fit the clock movement and hands.

WOOD AND PLASTER CLOCK

YOU WILL NEED

timber 15 - 20 mm (⅝ - ¾ in) thick,
and 80cm (32 in) long (the wood is
for the frame)

wood glue

card

glue

plaster of Paris

sandpaper

varnish

impact adhesive

clock movement and hands

*T*his extremely elegant clock is made from inexpensive basic
materials – plaster and wood.

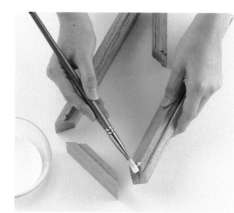

1 Plane a rebate into the wood to a
depth of 8 mm (⅓ in). Cut the wood
into four pieces (2 x 30 cm (12 in) and
2 x 10 cm (4 in)) to make a frame with
mitre corner joints. Stick together with
wood glue and leave to set overnight.

2 From pieces of cardboard make a
mould with a decorative base, to sit
inside the wooden frame. Waterproof
the mould by painting with a coat of
varnish. Leave to dry, and then clean
out the mould with a damp cloth.

3 Mix plaster of Paris by gradually
pouring water into a bowl of plaster.
Pour the plaster into the mould and
agitate to get rid of air bubbles. Leave
to set, before removing from the mould.

4 Sand the frame and, being careful
not to touch the rebate, varnish it.
Very carefully, drill a hole in the plaster for the clock fittings. Gently sand
the clock face to remove any blemish-
es. Apply any extra details such as
slivers of wood or card using impact
adhesive.

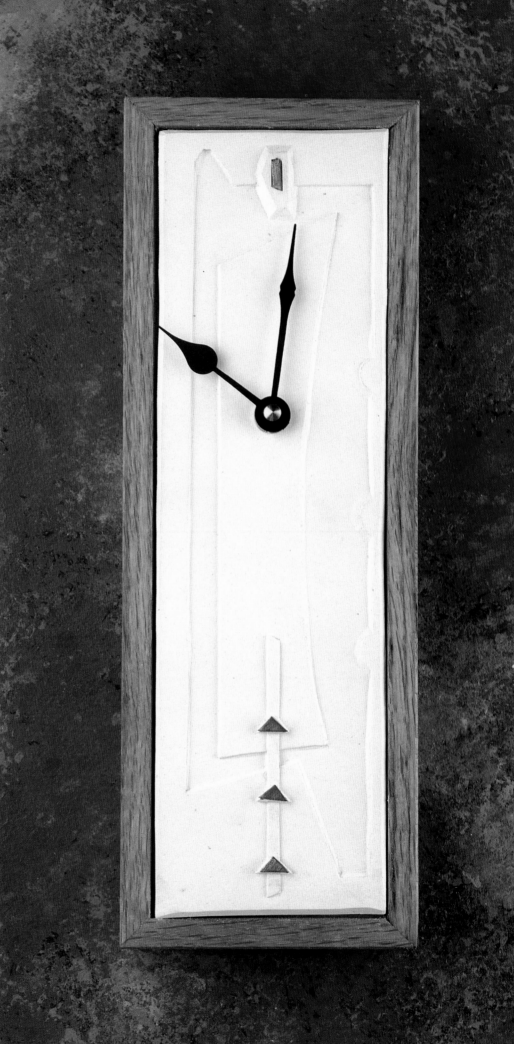

5 Using impact adhesive, stick the face inside the frame and fit the clock movement and hands.

NEEDLECRAFT CLOCKS

Fabric and threads may not instantly spring to mind as possible clock faces, but these colourful and attractive clocks feature a range of techniques from needlepoint and cross stitch, silk painting and appliqué, crochet and knitting.

NEEDLECRAFT CLOCKS GALLERY

*C*hild's cross stitch clock depicting events of the day to match the time. Even the numbers are worked in cross stitch. *Caroline Kelley*

*W*atermelon clock. This clock is made by crocheting synthetic raffia in a circle. Synthetic raffia is easier to use than natural raffia and the colours are more vibrant. *Rachel Marshall*

*P*anda clock. An unusual design but wonderful for a child's room made from fake fun fur with teddy bear eyes. The snout is fur backed by a small cheese box to keep it rigid and allow it to protrude. *Rachel Marshall*

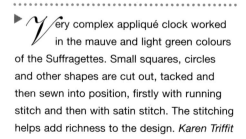

*V*ery complex appliqué clock worked in the mauve and light green colours of the Suffragettes. Small squares, circles and other shapes are cut out, tacked and then sewn into position, firstly with running stitch and then with satin stitch. The stitching helps add richness to the design. *Karen Triffit*

YOU WILL NEED

paper and pencil

tape measure

tracing paper

square of bronze-coloured velvet, 36 x 36 cm (14 x 14 in)

2 squares of metallic organza in cream and dark gold, each 36 x 36 cm (14 x 14 in)

dressmaker's pins

sewing needle, thread, machine

machine embroidery threads in black and gold

scissors

mounting board

pair of compasses

craft knife

latex adhesive and paintbrush

clock movement and hands

SUNBURST CLOCK

*T*his luxurious clock takes its inspiration from the styles favoured by Louis XIV, the Sun King.

1 Scale up the template provided so that it has a diameter of 30 cm (12 in). Trace onto tracing paper. Place the velvet square on a flat surface, and lay on top of it the square of dark gold organza, followed by the square of cream organza. Place the traced template in the centre of the fabric and pin and tack (baste) to secure.

2 Thread the sewing machine with gold thread and set to the widest satin stitch. Sew round the outer circle of the sun, joining all the layers of fabric together. Outline the main facial outline, the nostrils and the areas under the eyes in medium satin stitch, using gold thread.

4 Still working in black, outline the inner circle on the widest satin stitch setting. Change the setting to medium and outline the sun's rays.

5 Unpick the tacking (basting) and cut off the loose threads. Cut away the tracing paper.

6 Following the main picture, cut away one or two layers of the fabric to reveal the colours beneath.

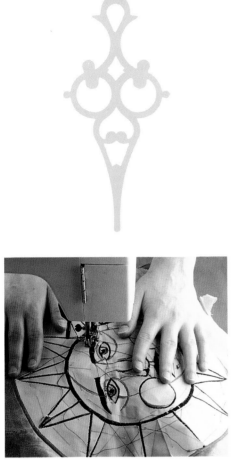

3 Using black thread and a single line of medium satin stitch, outline all the other features apart from the upper mouth and eyebrows as these need a double line.

7 Using a pair of compasses, draw a circle 30 cm (12 in) in diameter on mounting board.

8 Stick the fabric cloth onto the board using latex adhesive.

9 Cut a hole with a craft knife through the centre of the clock face. Push through the clock movement and attach the hands.

SILK PAINTED CLOCK

*S*ilk painting is a very popular method of decorating cloth. First a barrier of gutta is painted on, much the same as lead divides a stain glass window, then the colour is added.

1 Wash, dry and press the silk. Stretch it onto the wooden frame and pin in position. The fabric must be absolutely taut. Protect the work surface with heavy plastic. Using the template, draw the design in felt tip pen onto the tracing paper, allowing for a generous border all around the design.

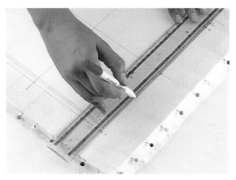

2 Secure the tracing paper underneath the silk frame with pieces of masking tape at each corner. Turn the silk frame over onto the table and draw with the vanishing textile marker, onto the silk, going over the design below.

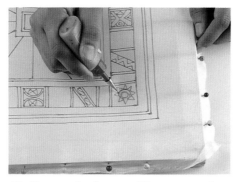

3 Now apply the metallic gutta to the outline of the design. This will block the mesh of the silk preventing the silk paint bleeding and merging. Allow the gutta to dry thoroughly.

4 Apply the silk paints taking care not to splash or go over any lines of gutta. Paint a plain border 2.5 cm (1 in) all around the design. Keep a tissue to hand to mop up any excess paint. Paint in the central pattern. Rectify small mistakes by using a cotton bud dipped in water. Allow the fabric to dry before removing from the frame.

5 Place the painted silk face down between two sheets of clean white paper and iron it according to the manufacturers instructions to fix paint. To assemble the clock, cut two pieces of heavy cardboard to the size of the finished design, excluding the plain border. Glue together and leave under a heavy object to dry for 24 hours.

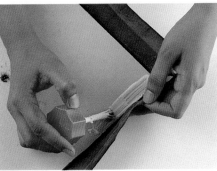

6 Trim the edges to fit the cardboard. Make a hole in the centre for the clock mechanism. Cut neatly around the silk design. Place the block on the back of the silk. Make sure that it is placed squarely on the painted area. Apply rubber based glue to the ends of the cardboard block and stretch the silk firmly over it. Leave to dry.

7 Cut a piece of silk slightly smaller than the block and stick it on the back of the block to cover the joins and neaten the edges. Trim the edges with fine braid. Make a hole in the centre of the design and attach the clock movement and hands.

SNAKES AND LADDERS CLOCK

*W*hen knitting the chequer board pattern, twist the navy and white yarns around each other when moving from one colour square to another.

To Knit the Chequerboard

Cast on 56 stitches in navy and knit 6 rows:

Row 1: k4(n), k8(w), k8(n), k8(w), k8(n), k8(w), k12(n).

Row 2: k4(n), p8(n), p8(w), p8(n), p8(w), k8(n), p8(w), k4(n).

Repeat these 2 rows 5 times.

Row 3: k12(n), k8(w), k8(n), k8(w), k8(n), p8(w), k4(n).

Row 4: k4(n), p8(w), p8(n), p8(w), p8(n), p8(w), p8(n), k4(n).

Repeat these 2 rows 5 times.

Begin with row 1 again and continue until there are 7 rows of checks. Knit 7 rows in navy and cast (bind) off loosely.

1 Turn over the work and sew in the ends. Press on the reverse side with a damp cloth to block into a square.

2 Using the chart provided, swiss darn the snakes and ladders in differing colours onto the knitted board. Use fly stitch for the tongues.

3 Work the numbers in chain stitch in the appropriate squares.

4 Find the centre of the clock face through the knitted board and using a craft knife cut a 10 mm (⅜ in) hole for the spindle in the card. Glue the knitted square to the card using latex adhesive. Fit the clock movement and hands.

ART DECO APPLIQUÉ

*T*his clock takes some time to finish but is well worth the effort.

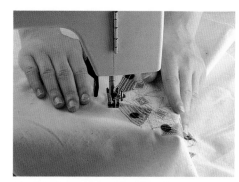

1 Stitch a circle of yellow linen 10cm (4 in) diameter in the centre of the calico. Using the main picture as a guide cut out all the shapes. Using satin stitch, stitch the star in the centre and the slightly larger triangles around the outside edge. Cut and stitch down copper satin triangles in between. Stitch small squares of gold fabric around the original circle, and tiny circles of black net at intervals on top of the outside triangles.

2 Arrange twelve squares of white velvet around the outside edge in a clock formation. Sew spirals on the inside of each square. In between, place triangles to fit this exact measurement. Stitch the triangles down using very close satin stitch in copper, then wider zig-zag stitch in white over the top. Make the copper satin band which the numerals will sit on. Stitch the copper coloured band into position. Cut the work away with a 3 cm (1⅛ in) turning allowance at the edge.

4 Cut out circles from black velvet and arrange between each square. Straight stitch, then satin stitch the circles into place. Finally decorate with white stitching on top.

5 Cut out 4 squares of gold satin approx 7 x 7 cm (2¾ x 2¾ in) and 8 small circles from yellow gingham. Back the squares and circles with calico. Pin the squares at 12, 3, 6 and 9 o'clock and the circles in between.

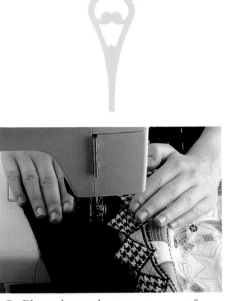

3 Place the work onto a square of black fabric (approx 55 cm x 55 cm (21¾ x 21¾ in)) and stitch down around the outside edge. Cut out a rim of black net to cover the 3 cm (1⅛ in) of calico. Make enough squares from black and white dogstooth (hounds-tooth) material and arrange diagonally across the top of the net. Sew first with straight stitch and then finish with satin stitch.

6 Sew all the pieces into place before cutting fine ribbon or piping cord to make the numerals and stitch these down. Cut the black fabric into a circle at least 5 cm (2 in) away from the black circles. Cut out a circle of card approx 47 cm (18 in) in diameter, or just slightly wider than the piece of work. Cut a hole in the centre of the card. Do the same with the fabric clock face. Place the fabric face down and glue up to about 11 cm (4¼ in) from the hole towards the outside edge.

7 Place the card on top, making sure the holes match. Pull the fabric over the outside edge of the cardboard and lace it across the back using strong string. Fit the clock movement and hands.

NEEDLEPOINT OCTAGONAL CLOCK

This colourful, symmetrical clock uses a variety of needlepoint stitches to great effect.

YOU WILL NEED
1 skein each of the following colours
in cotton pearl:
orange
red
purple
blue
light green
2 skeins of the following:
dark green
white
graph paper
22 gauge canvas - 25 cm (9½ in)
square
thin plywood 20 cm (7¾ in) square
⁷⁄₁₆th drill bit and drill
fret saw (scroll saw)
sandpaper
thread
black felt 20 cm (8 in) square
clock movement and hands

1 Draw to scale the diagram provided
onto graph paper, and trace this
onto the canvas using a dark pencil or
a ball point pen.

2 Following the colour guide provided, satin stitch the triangles chang-
ing the direction of the threads as you
work round the canvas. Use tent stitch
to cover the two rings. The large triangles are worked in bullion stitch and
the background filled in with basket
weave over four threads. When stitching the background, start and finish at
different points to avoid producing a
ridge.

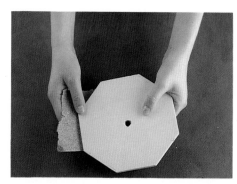

3 Cut the plywood into an octagon
slightly smaller than the original
plan. Drill a hole in the centre and
sand the edges.

4 Cut the canvas with a 2.5 cm (1 in)
border and stretch it over the wood
using double thread and a herring bone
stitch. Add extra thread as required by
tying on additional lengths. Ensure the
design is straight before pulling tight.

5 Cut the felt to shape and glue into position.

6 Make a cord from one skein of dark green cotton pearl and stitch invisibly to the edge. Fit the clock movement and hands.

COW JUMPED OVER THE MOON CLOCK

*C*ross stitch is used to adapt this traditional nursery theme into a clock.

YOU WILL NEED

14-gauge canvas, 25 x 40 cm (10 x 16 in)
sewing needle
black cotton thread
tape measure
stranded embroidery cotton in blue, turquoise, beige, rust, light green, pink, black, grey, brown, white, yellow and dark green
embroidery needle
scissors
pencil
thick plywood, 30 x 18 cm (12 x 7 in)
pair of compasses
fretsaw (scroll saw)
drill
sandpaper
strong thread
piece of felt, 30 x 18 cm (12 x 7 in)
latex adhesive
clock movement and hands

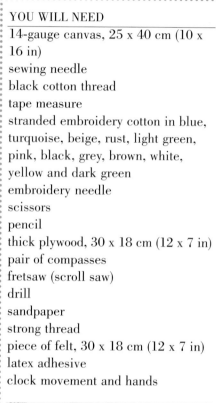

1 Tack (baste) a vertical line up the centre of the canvas and a horizontal line 5 cm (2 in) through from the bottom.

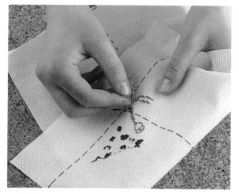

2 Using the chart provided as a guide, work the design in cross stitch using two strands of cotton. Outline the dog and the cow in double running stitch using a single strand of cotton.

3 Complete the picture before marking the position of the numerals in pencil. Work the motifs and numerals in cross stitch using two strands of thread.

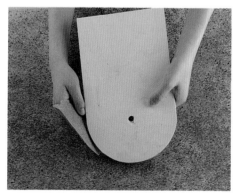

4 Using a pair of compasses, draw a curve at the top of the piece of plywood. Cut to shape using a fretsaw (scroll saw). Drill a hole in the centre for the spindle, and sand all edges until smooth.

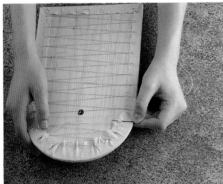

5 Cut the canvas to leave a 2.5 cm (1 in) border and stretch over the wood using a double length of strong thread and herringbone stitch. Add extra thread as required by tying on additional lengths. Make sure the design is straight before pulling tight.

6 Trim the felt shape and attach to the back with latex adhesive. When dry, fit the clock movement and hands.

BIRD OF PARADISE SAMPLER CLOCK

*F*or this project, use short lengths of wool of approximately 30 cm (12 in) to prevent wool thinning as it is passed through the canvas.

YOU WILL NEED
12-count tapestry canvas, 18 x 19 cm (7 x 7½ in)
pencil
ruler
tapestry needle
scissors
1 skein of tapestry wool in each of the following colours: red, dark blue, royal blue, green, light blue, purple, pale pink, orange, yellow and black
2 skeins of light green tapestry wool
green felt, 15 x 15 cm (6 x 6 in)
stiff card, 15 x 15 cm (6 x 6 in)
metal nut
sewing needle
extra strong thread
latex adhesive
pale green embroidery thread
clock movement and hands

1 Fold the canvas into 4, gently creasing along fold lines, and marking with pencil the point where the lines cross at right angles: this is the centre. Following the chart provided, draw in the outer edges of the sampler.

2 Using red wool, and following the chart, begin by stitching the numbers. Half-cross stitch is used throughout this sampler, each square on the chart represents one stitch. To start, tie a knot at the end of the wool, and take the needle from the front to the back of the canvas a little way from where the first stitch is made. Position the wool at the back so that the first 3 - 4 stitches cover and secure it. When secure, the knot at the front of the work can be cut off. This prevents bumps in the work when mounting. To finish, run the surplus wool through the back of the stitches for about 2.5 cm (1 in).

4 Mount the sampler on the piece of stiff card. Mark the centre point of the card. Bore a 10 mm (⅜ in) diameter hole through the centre with the scissors. Push the metal nut through the front sampler and the card, joining both together. Match the sides so that the card sits just inside the embroidered sampler.

Place the work face down on a clean surface. Fold back the surplus canvas ▶

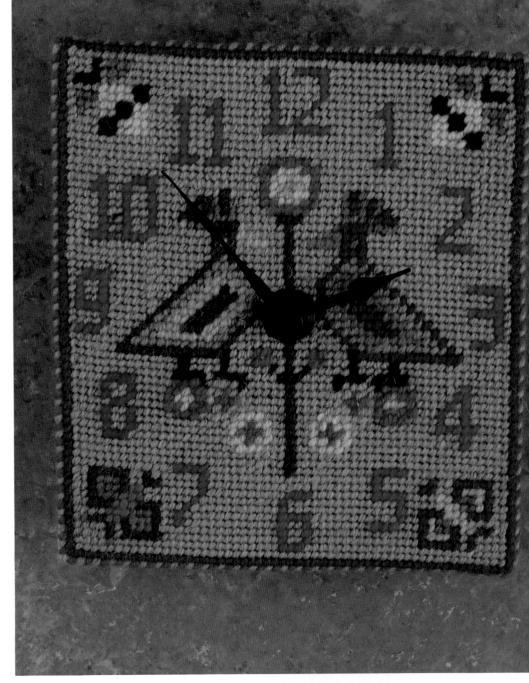

3 Next, work the bird, flower, butterfly and bee motifs. Fill in the background with light green wool, but do not stitch the centre 25 stitches. Finally, with needle and thread, sew the border rows. Carefully cut out the centre square of 9 stitches.

◀ at the sides of the work, so that it lies over the card. Using a needle and very strong thread, take long stitches from one side of the canvas to the other. Pull the stitches tightly, checking the front of the sampler now and then to make sure it is positioned correctly.

Fold back the surplus canvas at the top and bottom edges, lace in the same way as sides. Trim away any surplus canvas at each corner.

5 Take the piece of felt and mark the centre point. Snip out a 10 mm (⅜ in) diameter hole at this point. Match the top and side edges. Using latex adhesive, glue the felt to the back of the sampler. Place the sampler under some heavy books to dry flat. When dry, overstitch the two edges in a contrasting embroidery thread. Insert the clock movement and hands to complete the clock.

FLOWER CLOCK

*T*his clock does not require numerals as the 11 petals and stem mark the 12 points.

YOU WILL NEED
3.5 mm (E) crotchet hook
lengths of artificial raffia; yellow 30m (30 yards), orange 5m (5 yards), dark green 5m (5 yards)
10 m (10 yards) each of 11 different colours of raffia (1 for each petal)
round box lid (made from strong card or balsa wood) measuring approximately 11 cm (4½ in) in diameter, and approximately 2 cm (¾ in) in depth
35 cm (13½ in) thin wire
white paper 12 x 12 cm (4¾ x 4¾ in)
gold sticky tape 2.5 cm (1 in) wide
craft knife
dial template
tapestry needle
scissors
clock movement (long spindle) and hands
Note: Abbreviations in crochet patterns are explained on page 141.

1 Using a 3.5 mm (E) hook and yellow raffia crochet the clock face, working in rounds:

Round 1: 6 ch, sl st in first ch to form a ring. 1 ch, 11 dc into ring. Sl st in 1 ch at beginning of round.

Round 2: 1 ch, * 1 dc in first st, 2 dc in next st; rep from * 5 more times. Sl st in 1 ch at beginning of round.

Round 3: 1 ch, 1 dc in each of next 18 st. Sl st in ch at beginning of round.

Round 4: 1 ch* 1 dc, in first st, 2 dc in next st; rep from * 8 more times. Sl st in 1 ch at beginning of round.

Round 5: 1 ch, 1 dc in each st to end of round (27 st). Sl st in 1 ch at beginning of round. While crocheting this round, start with yellow raffia for 3 sts, then change to orange raffia and back to yellow every 3 sts throughout the round to give a flecked appearance.

Round 6: Using yellow raffia only, work 1 ch* 1 dc in first st, 2 dc in next st; rep from * 12 more times. 1 dc in last st. Sl st in 1 ch at beginning of round.

Round 7: Repeat 5th round (for 40 st instead of 27 st).

Round 8: Using yellow raffia only, work 1 ch, *1 dc in first st, 2 dc in next st; rep from * 19 more times. Sl st in 1 ch at beginning of round.

Round 9: Repeat 5th round (for 60 st instead of 27 st).

Round 10: Using yellow raffia only, work 1 ch, 1 dc in each of the next 60 st. Sl st in 1 ch at beginning of round.

Round 11: Begin to work the sides of the clock crocheting into the back loop only of each st: 1 ch, * 1dc in each of next 14 st, skip the following st; rep from *3 more times. Sl st in 1 ch, at beginning of round.

Round 12: 1 ch, 1 dc in each of next 56 st. Sl st into 1 ch, at beginning of round.

Round 13: Repeat 12th round.

Round 14: Repeat 12th round.

Round 15: 1 ch* 1 dc in each of next 13 st. Skip the following st; rep from * 3 more times. Sl st in 1 ch at beginning of round.

2 Cover the box sides (inside and out) and the top with gold sticky tape and trim edges neatly with a craft knife. Place the dial template on top of the box and bore a 10 mm (⅜ in) hole through the box with a pair of scissors. Fit the crocheted work over the box, matching the centre holes. Check that the sides of the crochet and the box are the same depth. If they are too short, repeat the 15th round until the crochet and box edges are the same depth, then work the 16th and 17th rounds.

Round 16: 1 ch * 1 dc in each of next 3 st, skip following st; rep from * 12 more times. Sl st in 1 ch at beginning of round. Trim away any long ends of raffia inside the work. Fit crochet work over the box.

Round 17: While the crochet is on the box, work the last round: 1 ch, 1 dc in each of next 39 sts. Fasten off. Sew in the end of the raffia.

3 Crochet 11 petals. For each petal use a different colour raffia. Work in rounds.

Round 1: 5 ch, sl st in first ch to form a ring. 1 ch, 12 dc into ring. Sl st in 1 ch at beginning of round.

Round 2: Sl st in each of first 3 st. 1 dc and 1 half tr in next st. 1 tr and 1 dtr in next st. 2 dtr in each of next 2 st. 1 dtr, and 1 tr in next st. 1 half tr and 1 dc in next st. 1 sl st in each of last 3 st.

Round 3: 1 sl st in each of first 5 sts. 1 dc and 1 half tr in next st. 1 tr and 2 dtrs in next st. 3 dtrs in each of next 4 sts. 2 dtrs and 1 tr in next st. 1 half tr and 1 dc in next st. Sl st in each of next 6 sts.

Round 4: 1 sl st in each of next 33 sts. (Crochet loosely so as not to distort the petal shapes). 2 ch. Fasten off, leaving an end of 40 cm (16 in).

4 To make the stem, place the dial template onto the crocheted clock face, lining up the centre points. At the 6 o'clock position, pierce two holes, one below the other, using the tapestry needle. Thread the wire evenly through the holes and twist both ends together. Using dark green raffia and a 3.5 mm (E) hook, crochet the stem as follows: Starting 20 cm (7¾ in) from the end of raffia make 1 ch.

Crocheting around the wire from the end of stem towards the clock face, work about 35 half trs, so that the wire is completely covered. Cut the raffia 40 cm (16 in) from the last half tr and fasten off. Thread this end onto a tapestry needle and stitch the stem to the clock face.

5 Stitch each of the 11 petals to the remaining points on the dial, using the long ends of raffia attached to each petal. Fasten off and trim all ends. Remove the template from the clock. Insert the movement and fit the hands to complete the clock.

FRENCH KNITTING CLOCK

YOU WILL NEED

knitting nancy or cord maker
3 skeins each of red, orange, yellow, green, blue and purple tapestry wool
white mounting board
pair of compasses
craft knife
drill
50 cm (½ yard) white cotton-polyester fabric
scissors
PVA glue
paintbrush
tapestry needle
dressmaker's pins
clock movement and hands

*F*rench knitting is quick and easy to produce and can be learnt by young children if they want to make the clock themselves.

1 Make lengths of French knitting in each of the colours long enough to fit around the circumference of the clock face (approximately 36 cm (14 in)). When you need to join in a second skein keep the knot to the inside.

2 Using a pair of compasses, draw a 36 cm (14 in) circle on mounting board and cut out with a craft knife. Drill a 10 mm (⅜ in) diameter hole in the middle. Cover one circle with cotton-polyester fabric notching the edge and sticking in position with PVA glue.

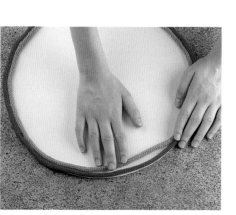

4 Repeat with the other colours, making them progressively shorter to fit inside the previous loop. Starting with the red loop, stick in position around the circle using PVA glue.

5 Mark the position of the numerals on the clock face with pins. Each finished number is 5 cm (2 in) high. Using different colours, cut lengths of French knitting to form numbers, finishing off by threading through all the loops and pulling the end back down the tube.

3 Position the red cord round the edge of the circle and overlap by about 10 mm (³⁄₈ in). Cut end and unravel slightly. Pull the finished end into the unravelled end and sew the ends together to make an invisible join. Trim the ends if necessary.

6 Stitch the 3, 6, 9, and 12 into shape before gluing. Use pins to hold all the numbers in position while the glue dries. Fit the clock movement and hands.

FUN
CLOCKS

Let your imagination run wild with these zany, crazy clock-faces. From magic wands to candy-coated clocks, here is a chance to create a clock that is truly unique. These innovative designs are sure to inspire and all have been created with easily obtainable materials that are simple to put together.

FUN CLOCKS GALLERY

They may look like space aliens, but they are in fact clocks on wheels. Tin has been cut into crazy shapes and then enamelled to create fun clocks.
Kim Ellwood and Mike Abbott

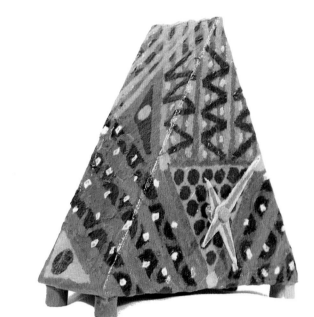

Clock on wheels with arms flailing in all directions. The spindly arms with the flowers or hands at the end are reminiscent of British children's cartoon comic characters from the Beano.
Kim Ellwood and Mike Abbott

A zany carriage clock made from hand-made paper. It has been decorated with layers of coloured paper with lots of swirls, circles and triangles completing the collage effect. *Gerry Copp*

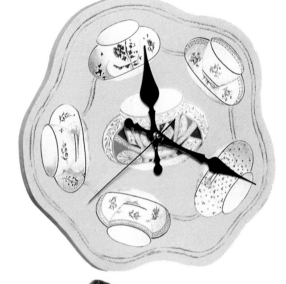

*T*his striking clock was painted a powder blue and decorated using teacup
motifs. *Josephine Whitfield*

*O*ld-fashioned Cuckoo clock made in
Germany. The bird noise is made by
tiny bellows at the back of the clock. The
man and woman swivel either side of the
barometer. The pattern on the clock is traditional folk-art flowers. *Author's Collection*

*B*lue fibre glass pig clock. Made
using a mould, the fibre glass is
built up in layers, then painted and given a
high gloss varnish. *Emma Clayton*

*F*ish clock made from steel plate decorated with brass. The background metal is scorched to produce a patented finish. *Richard Pell*

*S*teel has been cut into shape using metal (tin) snips. The octopus markings are then scorched onto the legs and body. The 12, 3, 6 and 9 are all marked with brass dots. *Richard Pell*

CANDY-SHAPED CLOCK

*T*his bright and cheerful clock would look good in a child's room - as long as it did not produce too many hunger pangs!

YOU WILL NEED

paper
pen
scissors
thin plywood
small saw
sandpaper
drill
pink acrylic paint
PVA glue
paintbrushes
assorted sweets and candies
assorted acrylic paints (optional)
clear polyurethane varnish
clock movement and hands

1 Scale up the template provided to the size required and transfer to paper. Cut out using scissors. Place on the piece of plywood and draw around it in pen.

2 Cut out the plywood base using a small saw and sand the edges smooth. Drill a hole in the centre to take the clock spindle. Paint the board using pink acrylic paint. Leave to dry.

3 Brush the board with PVA glue, covering a small area at a time as it is fairly fast-drying. Stick on the candies in your chosen arrangement. Continue until the clock is covered. Do not forget to leave a small space around the central hole.

4 Put 4 contrasting candies around the clock face for the numerals. When the PVA glue has dried, apply a coat of clear polyurethane varnish, taking care to brush it into all the gaps. Leave to dry, then fit the clock movement and hands. If you like, paint dots to the hands for extra decoration.

COLLAGE CLOCK

*T*hese exotic clocks are created from the simplest of household materials, yet look quite special.

1 Take a sheet of silver foil and crumple it up and flatten out again to give a crumpled appearance. Lay it face down and cover completely with double-sided tape. Cut the foil into a square, each side measuring twice the depth and once the width of the box, plus 2.5 cm (1 in). Draw a horizontal line the length of the foil equal to the depth measurement and 10 mm (⅜ in) in from the top edge. Draw a second line down the right-hand side of the square, 10 mm (⅜ in) in from the edge. Repeat along the bottom and the left-hand side of the square in the same way. This makes a grid of 9 squares. Cut away each corner square to leave a cross shape. Put the corners to one side.

2 Remove the top layer of double-sided tape from the foil cross to reveal the sticky side. Place the box face down onto the central square of the foil cross, matching the box and foil corners.

4 Select images from magazines or wrapping paper and cut them out roughly. Cover the back with double-sided tape and re-cut the pictures neatly. Arrange the pictures, around the box, remove the backing from the tape and press the motifs into place.

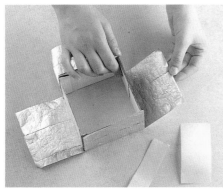

3 Press the foil on firmly. Smooth each foil panel down onto the sides and over the edges to the inside of the box. If any areas on the outside are not covered properly, cut strips from one of the extra corners to patch them up.

5 Mark the centre point of the clock face using a pair of compasses. Bore a 10 mm (³⁄₈ in) hole through the box, push the nut through the hole from the inside of the box. Cut away the excess card with a craft knife from the base of the nut. Paint the box with 2 coats of clear polyurethane varnish, allowing to dry between coats.

6 Mark the position of the numbers using a clock face template. Stick or transfer the numerals onto white paper leaving 10 mm (³⁄₈ in) between each. Cover the back of the paper with double-sided tape. Cut out each numeral leaving a circle of white paper around it. Stick the numbers into place on the clock front.

7 Attach the feet by making holes in the box and threading the wire through the beads and securing. Paint the clock hands with blue enamel paint. Leave to dry then fit the hands and the clock movement.

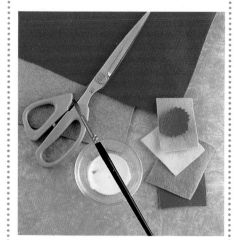

FELT CLOCK

*F*elt is an excellent craft medium - the choice of colours is wide, and the fabric does not fray and can be easily glued in place.

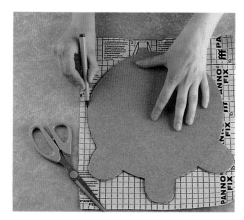

1 Using a pair of compasses, draw a circle 25 cm (10 in) in diameter onto a piece of cardboard. Add 3 bumps on the top of the circle. Cut out using a craft knife. Place the cardboard base on the back of the self-adhesive felt and draw round it. Cut out the felt with scissors.

2 Peel the backing paper off the felt and stick it down on top of the cardboard base.

3 Cut out an assortment of felt circles and in a variety of sizes, cutting some with pinking shears to give a decorative edge. Cut out 4 small hearts. Stick the shapes on the bumps using latex adhesive.

4 Arrange more circles and the hearts on the clock face in the position of the numbers 3, 6, 9 and 12, and stick down. Stick small felt dots cut using a hole punch onto the face of the clock.

5 Pierce a hole in the centre of the clock face with the point of the scissors. Fit the clock movement and hands.

CRAZY WALL CLOCK

*T*his bright clock puts to good use the coloured foil wrappers from chocolate assortments.

YOU WILL NEED
- pencil
- paper
- cardboard
- scissors
- masking tape
- old newspapers
- wallpaper paste
- water
- string
- PVA glue
- paintbrushes
- ready-made gesso
- coloured foil
- assorted acrylic paints
- clear acrylic varnish
- clock movement and hands

1 Scale up the template provided and transfer to the cardboard. Cut out using scissors.

2 Pierce a hole in the centre of the front to take the spindle. Stick the pieces together using masking tape. Screw up newspaper into 6 balls and then tape them onto the sides of the clock.

4 Leave to dry and then repeat with another 3 coats of papier-mâché. When dry, stick string on the clock in patterns using PVA glue.

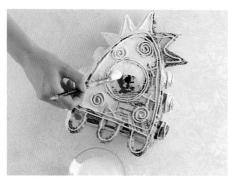

5 When dry, paint the whole clock with a coat of ready-made gesso and leave to dry once again.

6 Rub coloured foil onto the patterned areas and stick into position using PVA glue. Cut off any excess foil.

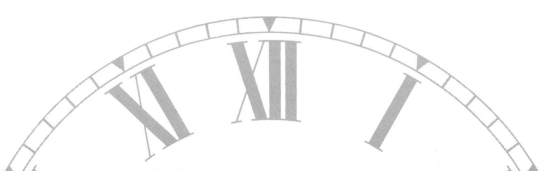

3 Make up the wallpaper paste according to the manufacturer's instructions. Tear the newspaper into strips and dip into the paste. Cover the clock with strips of papier-mâché making sure the balls and the crown on top of the clock are well covered.

7 Highlight the ridges in the foil in black acrylic paint. Paint in the clock face and, when dry, apply a coat of clear acrylic varnish. Cover short lengths of string in coloured foil and use to hang the suspended motifs from the bottom of the clock. Fit the clock movement and hands.

WINDOW BOX CLOCK

*P*lace this unusual clock on a sunny windowsill and watch the plants grow as time passes.

YOU WILL NEED

plastic window box
tape measure
pair of compasses
craft knife
pencil
self-adhesive numerals
gravel
clock movement and hands
extra washers, if required
small plants in pots

1 Measure the centre of the window box with a tape measure. Draw a circle 10 mm (³⁄₈ in) in diameter and another 9 cm (3½ in) in diameter. Cut out the smaller circle using a craft knife.

2 Mark the position of the numerals in pencil round the larger circle ensuring they are evenly distributed.

3 Trim the numerals as necessary and press firmly in position on the clock face area.

4 Pour a layer of gravel 2.5 cm (1 in) deep into the base of the window box. Dampen slightly with water.

5 Fit the clock movement and hands using the extra washers if required and place the plants in their pots on the gravel. Put on a sunny windowsill. When watering, take care not to get the clock movement and battery wet.

MAGIC WAND CLOCK

A delightful clock for an adult or child, made from copper sheet and wire on a base of self-hardening clay.

YOU WILL NEED

metal (tin) snips
copper wire
copper sheet
pair of compasses
ruler
thin card
craft knife
pliers
fretsaw (scroll saw)
10 mm (³⁄₈ in) diameter aluminium tube, 40 cm (16 in) in length
self-hardening clay
rolling pin
sharp modelling tool
terracotta-coloured acrylic paint
paintbrushes
clear acrylic varnish
gold powder pigment
clock movement and hands

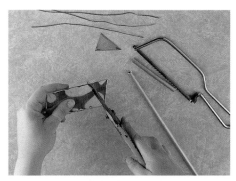

1 Using metal (tin) snips, cut 5 pieces of copper wire 20 cm (8 in) long, and 4 pieces 18 cm (7 in) long. Cut 5 triangles and 1 heart from the copper sheet, following the templates provided. Draw a circle of 11.5 cm (4½ in) in diameter on a piece of card. Draw a second circle within this to a diameter of 6 cm (2¼ in) and cut out.

2 Using pliers, bend the shorter pieces of wire into zig-zag shapes and 4 of the longer ones into spirals. Bend the top ends of the wire over slightly. Using a fretsaw (scroll saw), cut the aluminium tube into 2 pieces, one piece measuring 10 cm (4 in), the other 30 cm (12 in).

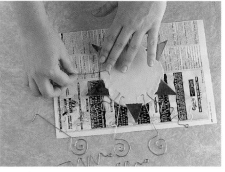

4 While the clay is still wet, embed the copper triangles around the edge of the solid circle. Stick the zig-zag wires and the spirals into the clay, alternating them between the triangles. Place the shorter aluminium tube at the bottom of the circle and place the hollow disc on top so that it fits flush with the solid one below. Press together gently and remove the tube.

5 Roll out the clay again and cut 2 hexagons. Bend a length of copper wire into a loop and insert between the two hexagons. Insert the bottom end of the longer aluminium tube into the other end. Press the clay layers together. Press the metal heart into the centre of the top hexagon. Make a hole for the spindle and leave all parts of the clock to dry for 2 - 3 days.

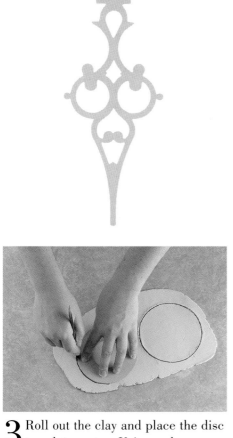

3 Roll out the clay and place the disc template on top. Using a sharp modelling tool, cut 2 discs, one using the outer edge only, the other including the inner circle as well.

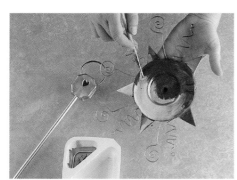

6 When dry, prime the clay with terracotta-coloured acrylic paint. Leave to dry. Mix clear acrylic varnish with gold powder pigment and paint over the terracotta-coloured areas and the tube. Fit the clock movement and hands and, to finish, wind wire up around the aluminium tube to decorate.

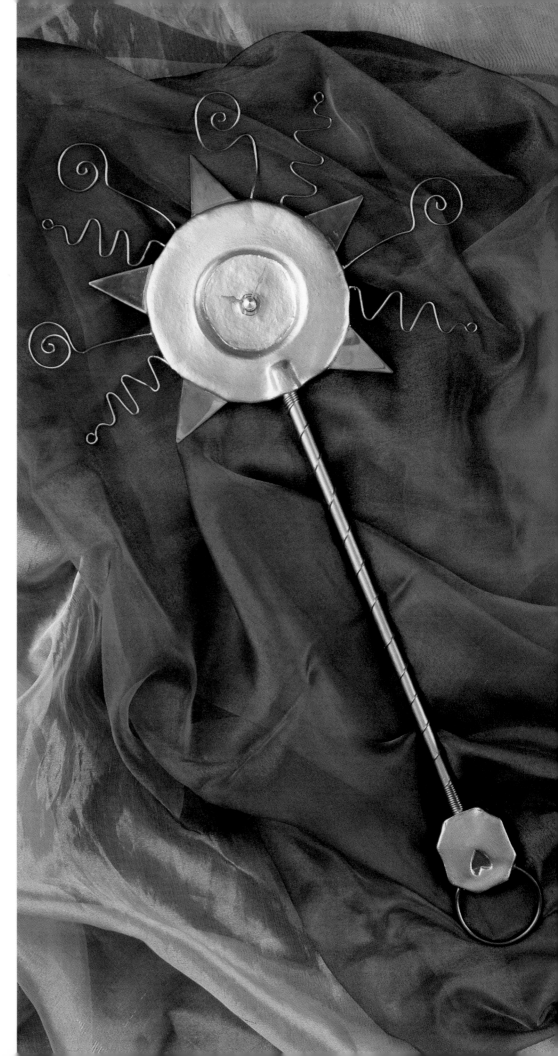

PIG CLOCK

*T*his amusing clock is ideal for a child's room. Experiment with the features and colours to make other animals.

YOU WILL NEED

thin card
pair of compasses
craft knife
small round box or box lid
pencil
masking tape
50 cm (½ yard) pale pink fake fur
50 cm (½ yard) bright pink felt
scissors
sewing needle
sewing thread
dressmaker's pins
scraps of black and yellow felt
latex adhesive
1 pair large orange safety eyes
clock movement and hands

1 Using a pair of compasses, draw a circle measuring 25 cm (10 in) in diameter onto thin card. Cut out using a craft knife. Place the small box on the card circle about one-third in from one edge and draw round in pencil.

2 Using a craft knife, cut away the card from the smaller circle.

4 Using the template provided as a guide, cut out 2 outer ears in pale pink fake fur, and 2 inner ears in bright pink felt. Also cut out a fake fur circle 25 cm (10 in) in diameter. Measure the small box and cut out a felt cover for the nose, and a fake fur strip to go around the sides of the nose. With right sides together, tack (baste) one fake fur ear to one felt ear around the curved sides. Sew as close to the edges as possible. Turn the ear the right way out.

3 To make the base for the pig's nose, insert the small box into the hole and fix it all the way round on the inside with masking tape.

5 With right sides together, tack (baste) the nose to the head circle. Sew to secure. Make a hole for the spindle in the centre of the nose.

6 Stick the face in place over the circle and small box using latex adhesive. Cut out nostrils, a mouth and eyelashes from black felt, and lips from the remaining pink felt. Cut 2 eye circles from yellow felt and glue in position using latex adhesive. Push the safety eyes through the felt and fur and fix in place with latex adhesive. Fit the clock movement behind the nose and add the hands.

BASIC TECHNIQUES

*T*he designs in this book offer plenty of opportunity to try out new craft skills. This section offers general advice on those techniques and specific examples of the individual stitches required to complete the needlecraft designs.

RESIZING A DESIGN

All the projects in this book are provided with a design or template. Sometimes a design is the right size, but more often you will need to enlarge or reduce it. Using a photocopying machine with that facility is easiest, although enlargements of more than 156 per cent may involve two stages, making a second enlargement of the first copy.

You can also draw a squared grid over the original design, then, on a second sheet of paper, make a larger or smaller grid, with the same number of squares. (With any of the designs in this book, trace it onto a sheet of tracing paper first, then draw a grid over it.) Mark onto the new grid the points where the original design bisects the original grid lines, square by square, then connect up the lines. If any of the

lines look awkward or disjointed, don't be afraid to improvise a little, smoothing out the curves. To double the size of a design, overlay a 2.5 cm (1 in) square grid on the original, then redraw it on a 5 cm (2 in) square grid. To halve the size, re-draw it on a 1.25 cm (½ in) square grid. You can also change the proportions of the design, by increasing or decreasing the horizontal or vertical lines unequally.

TRANSFERRING A DESIGN

Once you have your design on paper, you will need to transfer it to your clock face. Cut a square or rectangle of tracing paper and a similar sized one of carbon paper to give a margin of at least 2.5 cm (1 in) around the design. Trace your design onto the tracing paper. Place the carbon paper, carbon-side down, onto the surface area to be

decorated. Position the tracing paper on top and stick both in place with small pieces of masking tape, to prevent accidental movement while the design is transferred. Using a sharp pencil, draw over the tracing, pressing firmly and evenly to ensure that the carbon adheres to the surface. If you are repeating the pattern, slightly move the carbon paper each time so an unused area is beneath the tracing.

DÉCOUPAGE TECHNIQUES

Découpage is a way of decorating almost any object or surface with cut-out pieces of paper to achieve a pictorial or abstract design. The materials and equipment you will need for découpage are inexpensive and easy to obtain from arts and crafts shops. After the paper pieces are applied, the design is sealed and protected with several coats of varnish.

CHOOSING MATERIALS
Decorative images for découpage are all around you in the form of magazines, old greetings cards, wrapping paper, picture postcards, illustrated catalogues and paper packaging. Photocopies work well too - colour ones just need cutting out and applying, while black and white copies can

be hand-coloured or used as they are to create striking monochrome designs. Tissue paper, coloured and hand-made paper give interesting effects - tissue paper can look almost translucent when given several coats of varnish.

PREPARING SURFACES

Surfaces for découpage need to be clean, dry and smooth. Clean old metal objects with heavy-duty steel (wire) wool, then rinse in a solution of one part water to one part vinegar. Use the same solution to rinse new metal. Metal objects may also need two coats of rust-resistant paint. Wooden surfaces should be lightly sanded, then wiped with white spirit. Seal porous surfaces with matt emulsion (flat latex) paint; wipe down glass and ceramic surfaces to remove grease and dust.

CUTTING OUT

At times it may be easier to cut out shapes roughly using large scissors and leave a generous margin round the image. Change to small scissors to cut out the details. You may prefer to use a craft knife and cutting mat for intricate designs.

STICKING THE SHAPES IN POSITION

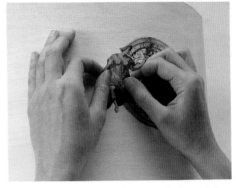

Use PVA glue at full strength for sticking down shapes. Tweezers are useful for picking up and positioning small, delicate cut-out shapes while scissors are useful when handling larger pieces. Check that all the shapes are stuck down well before varnishing and add extra glue where necessary. When the pieces have been stuck down, cover with a slightly damp cloth and press with a roller to remove air bubbles.

VARNISHING

Make sure the découpage is thoroughly dry before varnishing. You can use anything between two and 20 coats of varnish, allowing each layer to dry in a dust-free place. The more coats of varnish you apply, the smoother the surface of the finished object will feel to the touch. Between coats, sand the surface lightly, then wipe with a damp cloth.

Use PVA glue diluted two parts water to one part PVA or a clear polyurethane wood varnish (choose a non-toxic type). Artist's acrylic varnish

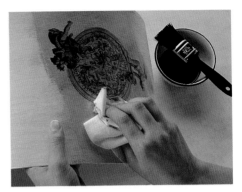

is more expensive, but it will not yellow with age. Varnishes containing coloured stains can be used to make a piece of découpage look old. A decorative effect can be achieved with crackle varnish, or two varnishes used together to create a decoratively cracked and crazed surface, colouring the cracks with artist's oil paints.

PAPIER-MÂCHÉ TECHNIQUES

MATERIALS

Papier-mâché is the art of modelling with torn or shredded paper bound together with glue, usually a water-based variety. The skills of papier-mâché are very quick to master and offer endless variation. Only readily available materials and equipment are required: newspaper or coloured craft paper, glue, large bowls or dishes, and masking tape. The most convenient adhesive to bind papier-mâché is PVA glue. This is non-toxic and can be diluted with water to give different strengths. It dries very quickly to leave a strong surface that will hold paint well.

SHREDDING PAPER

Old newspapers are excellent for papier-mâché. Tear them along the grain of the paper - the direction in which tearing is easiest - into strips approximately 2.5 - 5 cm (1 - 2 in) wide. Do not worry about creating ragged edges when you tear as these give a smoother finish to the object. Coloured papers can also be used, and give a decorative mosaic effect. Tear an assortment of colours into rough squares, approximately 2.5 cm (1 in) in size. The colours can be alternated when glued down. Again, rough edges are an advantage, both in producing a smooth finish and in creating a pleasantly mottled appearance.

MOULDS AND FRAMEWORKS
Almost any object can be used as a mould for papier-mâché, although rounded surfaces are easier to cover smoothly if the mould is to be removed later. Bowls or large dishes are excellent and one side can be covered to create a replica of the shape.

Before applying papier-mâché to a mould, ensure the mould is first greased with a liberal coating of petroleum jelly so that it can be removed easily when dry.

BUILDING UP THE SHAPE
Soak the pieces of paper one by one as you need them in diluted PVA glue. If covering a mould or framework, lay on the strips individually, working from top to bottom of the shape, with the strips running in the same direction.

When the first layer is complete, apply another, this time running in the opposite direction to provide extra strength.

Apply about four layers in all, more if you want your construction to be particularly strong. As a final touch, it is useful to brush a coat of glue over the layers using a large paintbrush.

DRYING
When modelling is complete, leave the papier-mâché to dry thoroughly. Leave in a warm place such as an airing cupboard, preferably overnight. Do not leave near a direct heat source as this may cause the papier-mâché to bend and warp.

DECORATION
When the papier-mâché is dry, gently remove the mould, if one has been used. If you want a neat finish, trim and re-cover the rough edges where the paper pieces overlapped. Sometimes, however, these uneven finishes can be very decorative, on the rim of a bowl for example.

If you are painting your object, prime with two coats of white paint, leaving the first coat to dry before applying the second. This will conceal any newsprint that may show through the colours. Both poster paints and acrylics are ideal for colouring papier-mâché and all types of decoration can be applied from freehand designs, sponging and stippling to the addition of 'gems' and metallic braid.

To give papier-mâché a shiny finish coat with clear non-toxic varnish.

APPLIQUÉ TECHNIQUES

WORKING MACHINE APPLIQUÉ
Always work a small practice piece before starting to machine stitch or machine appliqué in order to check that your thread, needle, stitch size and fabric are compatible. Fit a new needle before starting to sew as a blunt one will damage the fabric and result in uneven stitching.

SATIN STITCH
To work satin stitch, set your machine to a zigzag stitch about 3 mm (⅛ in)

wide and 6 mm (¼ in) long. Use a special appliqué foot if one is provided with your machine. Test the stitch on a spare piece of fabric, practising points and corners, and adjust your machine as necessary. A piece of typing paper placed beneath your fabric on top of the sewing machine plate will help when puckering is a problem - stitch the design then tear away the paper.

Start stitching at the beginning of a straight edge and do not go too fast. When working intricate shapes, go carefully and turn the wheel by hand to make one stitch at a time. Pivot at the corner of shapes by leaving the needle in the fabric, raising the presser foot and turning the fabric before lowering the foot and continuing to stitch. Never turn the wheel of the machine backwards as this will damage the machine.

KNITTING & CROCHET TECHNIQUES

KNITTING ABBREVIATIONS
k = knit
p = purl
st(s) = stitch(es)
beg = beginning
inc = increase
tog = together
st st = stocking stitch
** = instructions shown between the asterisks must be repeated

KNIT STITCH
With the yarn at the back of the work, insert the right-hand needle through the first stitch on the left-hand needle, wind the yarn over the right-hand needle, pull through a loop, then slip the original stitch off the left-hand needle. Repeat along the row until all the stitches have been transferred to the right-hand needle.

EMBROIDERING OVER KNITTING
Thread a blunt darning needle with the yarn. Insert the needle from back to front of the work at the centre of the first stitch to be embroidered over, taking care not to split the knitted stitches. Insert the needle behind both threads of the stitch above, then through the next two strands below. Take care to keep the tension of the embroidered stitches the same as that of the knitting so that your work does not pucker. If the embroidery is to cover several rows, complete one row as described above, and insert the needle under the upper loop of the last stitch. Turn the work upside down and embroider across the next row.

CROCHET ABBREVIATIONS
sl st = slip stitch
ch = chain stitch
dc = double crochet (US single crochet)
tr = treble (US double crochet)
dtr = double treble (US treble crochet)
rep = repeat
st(s) = stitch(es)
* = stitches shown after this sign must be repeated from this point
( ) = the stitch combination enclosed in brackets must be repeated in the order shown.

THE BASIC STITCHES

CHAIN STITCH
Wrap the yarn over the hook (a) and draw the yarn through to make a new loop (b).

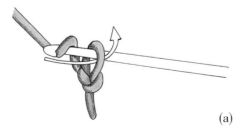
(a)

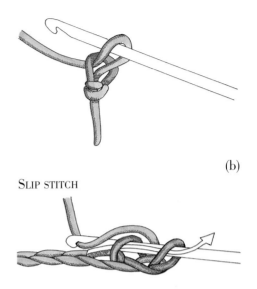
(b)

SLIP STITCH

Insert the hook in the work, wrap the yarn over the hook, then draw the yarn through both the work and the loop on the hook in one movement.

DOUBLE TREBLE (US TREBLE CROCHET)
Wrap the yarn over the hook twice and insert the hook in the work (a), wrap the yarn over the hook and draw the yarn through the work only (b) so there are now four loops on the hook, wrap the yarn again and draw the yarn through the first two loops on the hook

(a)

(b)

(c)

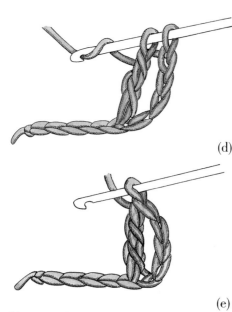

(d)

(e)

(c), wrap the yarn and draw the yarn through the next two loops only (d), wrap the yarn and draw through the remaining two loops on the hook (e).

DOUBLE CROCHET (US SINGLE CROCHET)

(a)

(b)

Insert the hook in the work, wrap the yarn over the hook and draw the yarn through the work only (a) so there are now two loops on the hook, wrap the yarn again and draw the yarn through both loops on the hook (b).

TREBLE CROCHET (US DOUBLE CROCHET)
Wrap the yarn over the hook and insert the hook in the work (a), wrap the yarn over the hook and draw the yarn

(a)

(b)

(c)

(d)

through the work only (b) so there are now four loops on the hook, wrap the yarn again and draw the yarn through the first two loops on the hook (c), wrap the yarn and draw the yarn through the remaining two loops on the hook (d).

CROSS STITCH TECHNIQUES

USING STRANDED COTTON
Most of the projects in this book are embroidered with stranded cotton. This consists of six separate strands of thread loosely twisted together. When a project requires two or three strands, first cut a length about 38 cm (15 in) long from the skein, then separate all six strands and combine them once again to give the required thickness (for the required number of strands).

CROSS STITCH CANVAS
Cross stitch fabrics come in various mesh sizes, or 'counts'. If the size specified in a pattern is not available, use the next size up or down. The design will appear slightly enlarged or condensed but the pattern itself will not be distorted.

STARTING AND FINISHING
Do not begin with a knot at the end of your thread as this can cause an unsightly lump when your project is finished, or it may work loose and cause the stitching to unravel. Instead, secure your thread by making one or two stitches in a space which will be covered by the embroidery. When the length of thread is nearly used up, slide the needle under a group of stitches on the wrong side for about 1 cm (½ in) to anchor the thread, then cut off the loose end. You can also use this method to secure a new thread in a group of existing stitches to continue a project.

WORKING FROM A CHART

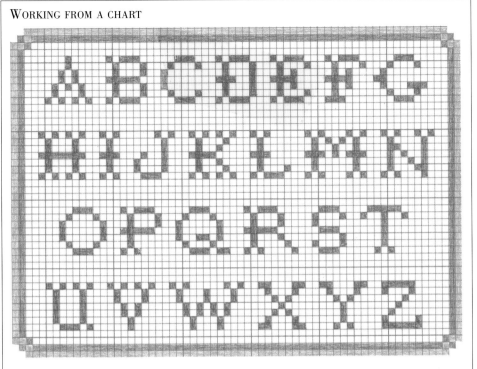

Read the instructions carefully before you begin to stitch. These will tell you how to mark the position of the embroidery on the fabric, and at which point on the chart you should begin stitching from. You will need to mark your starting point on the chart with a soft pencil so that the mark can be erased later.

Begin stitching from the correct point and work outwards, remembering that each coloured square on the chart represents one cross stitch to be embroidered on the fabric. The instructions will also tell you the number of woven fabric blocks you need to cover with each stitch so that the design will be the correct size.

To secure the work in the hoop, spread the fabric, right side up, over the smaller hoop and press the larger hoop over the top. Tighten the screw lightly, then gently pull the fabric with your fingers until it is evenly stretched. Tighten the screw fully to hold the fabric in place.

On large projects, you will need to move the hoop along after one portion of the design has been completed. Protect the embroidery already worked by spreading white tissue paper over the right side of the fabric before it is remounted in the hoop. Tear away the paper to expose the next area to be stitched.

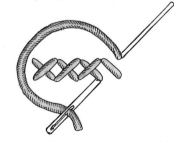

CROSS STITCH

There is more than one method of working cross stitch, but you should remember that the top diagonal stitches of each cross should always slant in the same direction, usually from bottom left to top right.

USING AN EMBROIDERY HOOP

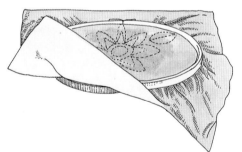

An embroidery hoop will help you to stitch more evenly and help prevent distortion to the fabric. A hoop consists of two rings placed one inside the other with the fabric sandwiched tightly in

between. The rings are secured by a screw on the outer ring.

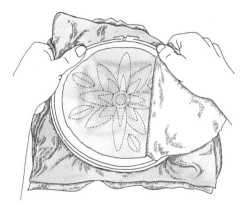

Use the first method for working individual stitches and small details on the designs, making sure you complete

each cross before proceeding to the next one.

Use the second method for embroidering cross stitch over large areas as it will help you to achieve a more evenly stitched result. Begin by working a row of diagonal stitches from right to left, then complete the crosses with a second row of diagonal stitches worked in the opposite direction.

HALF CROSS STITCH

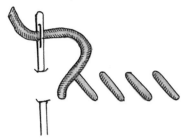

If you work just the bottom diagonal stitches, using either of the two methods shown, the stitch is then called half cross stitch.

NEEDLEPOINT STITCHES
. . . .

TENT STITCH
There are two methods of working tent stitch:

Use the diagonal method shown in the top stitches for working large areas as this method is less likely to pull the canvas out of shape. Work up and down in diagonal rows, making small diagonal stitches over one intersection of the canvas.

Use the second method for embroidering details and single lines. Begin at the lower edge of the shape and work in horizontal rows as shown in the bottom stitches.

BULLION KNOT STITCH

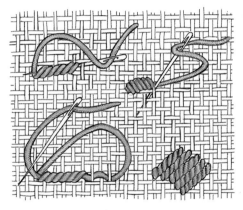

Bullion knots provide useful detail on pictorial work. Bring the needle out and push it in further over. Bring it out where the thread emerges to set the length of the stitch. Do not pull the needle all the way through. Wrap the thread around the needle as many times as the length requires. Hold the twists with your thumb and pull the needle through the canvas and the twists. Pull the needle and twists back the other way so that the coil lies flat. Push the needle back in and over to where the stitch began.

BASKETWEAVE STITCH
Basketweave stitch looks exactly the same on the front as Tent Stitch except that it is stitched in a different way. It is good for covering large background areas especially where there are few colour changes and causes a minimum amount of distortion to the canvas.

This stitch consists of diagonal stitches worked over one thread of the canvas from one corner. Make several stitches up and then several across each time as on the diagram.

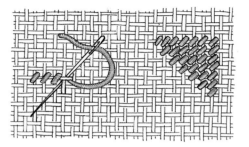

HERRINGBONE STITCH
Herringbone stitch is a dense and hard-wearing stitch which is ideal for footstools or rugs. When worked over large areas an attractive texture is achieved. This stitch is worked in rows across the canvas.

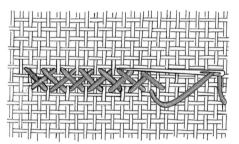

Work the stitch from left to right. Bring the thread out, take it up diagonally and make a short back stitch on the top line. Repeat making a similar stitch at the bottom line, bringing needle out directly under starting point above. Complete the row in this way. Work further rows one thread directly below the first one in the same way.

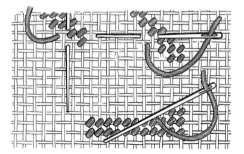

EMBROIDERY STITCHES

FLY STITCH

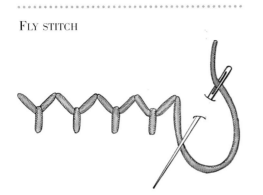

DOUBLE RUNNING STITCH

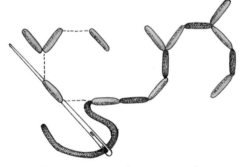

Fly stitch is an isolated stitch often worked in rows. Each stitch is worked very easily; a V-shaped loop is made and then tied down with a vertical straight stitch. The tying stitch can vary in length to produce different effects. The fly stitches can be arranged side by side to make a horizontal row, or worked underneath each other to make a vertical row. The stitches can touch one another or be spaced apart at regular intervals. Isolated fly stitches can be used to make a pretty powdering, either spaced evenly or randomly scattered over a shape. Each stitch can be decorated by the addition of a Chinese knot in a contrasting thread. Any type of thread can be used for this stitch, although stitch size and fabric weight must be taken into account.

Double running stitch is extremely easy to work and is a useful stitch, both for outlines and for intricate linear details. It is worked in two operations. Begin by working evenly spaced running stitches on the traced line. Then using the same or contrasting coloured thread, work running stitches in the spaces left. Unlike back stitch, double running stitch is quite reversible.

CHAIN STITCH

Bring needle out and make a straight stitch downwards inserting the needle at the starting point. Pull through with loop under needle point. Repeat, inserting needle where thread emerges. Finish row with a small stitch over last chain loop to secure.

SNAKES AND LADDERS CLOCK

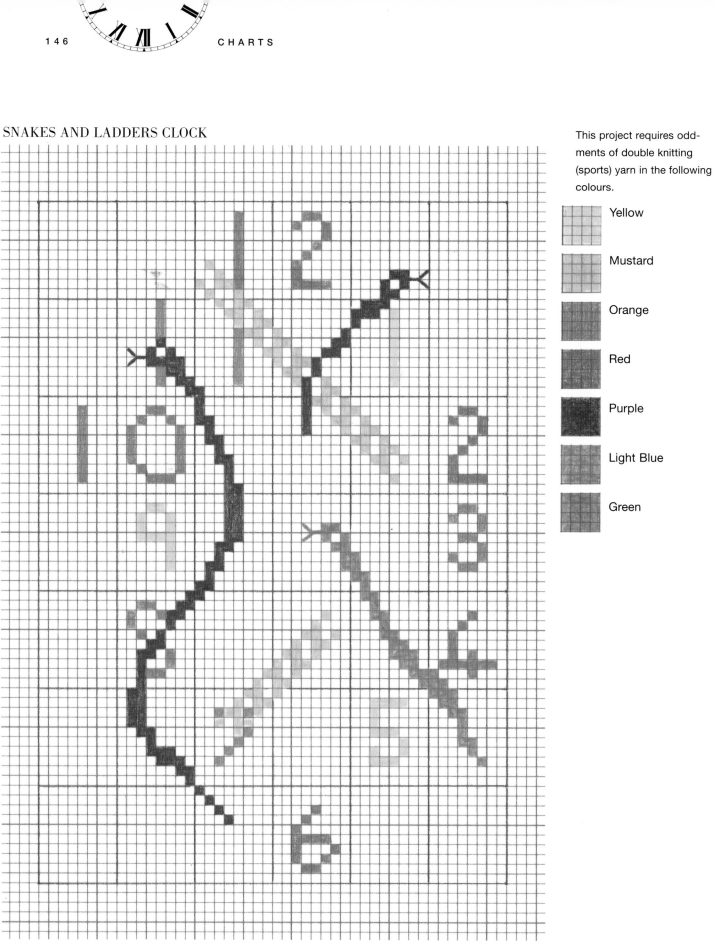

This project requires odd-ments of double knitting (sports) yarn in the following colours.

Yellow

Mustard

Orange

Red

Purple

Light Blue

Green

NEEDLEPOINT OCTAGONAL CLOCK

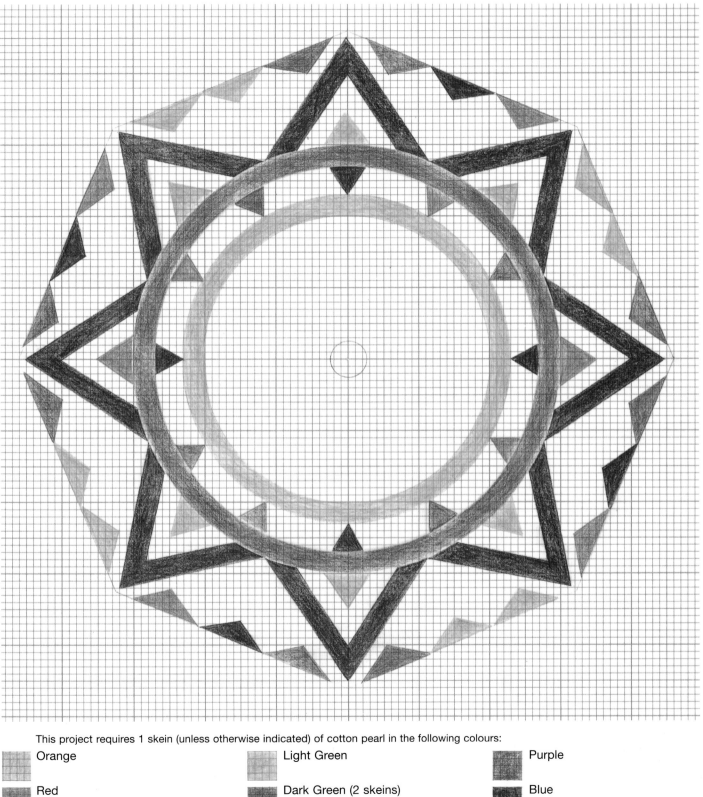

This project requires 1 skein (unless otherwise indicated) of cotton pearl in the following colours:

Orange

Red

Light Green

Dark Green (2 skeins)

Purple

Blue

COW JUMPED OVER THE MOON CLOCK

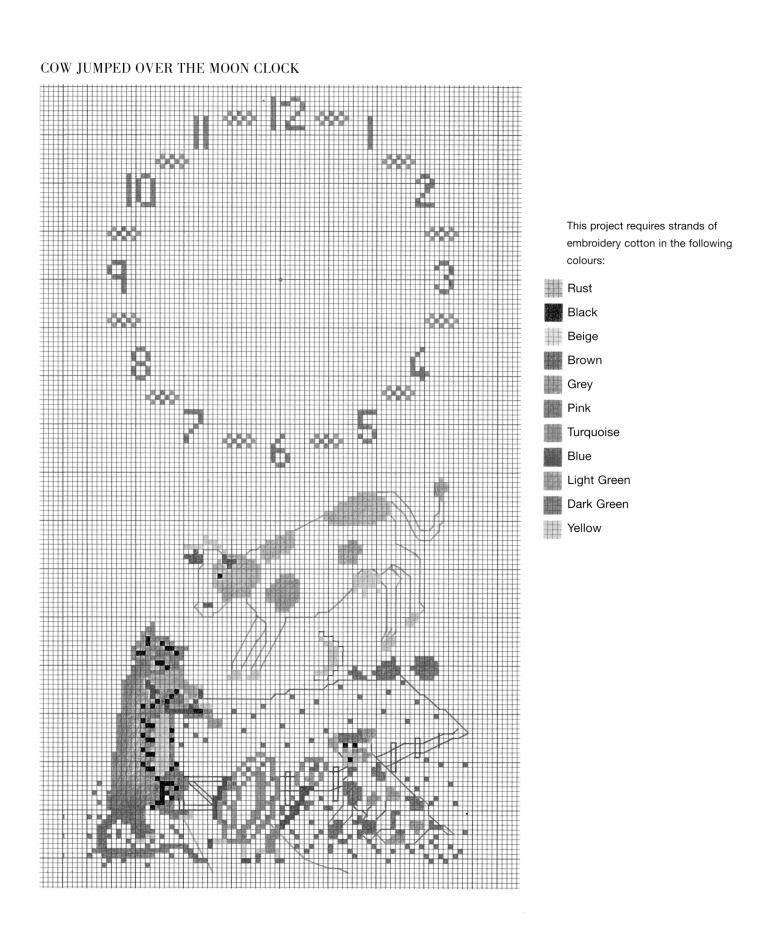

This project requires strands of embroidery cotton in the following colours:

Rust
Black
Beige
Brown
Grey
Pink
Turquoise
Blue
Light Green
Dark Green
Yellow

BIRD OF PARADISE CLOCK

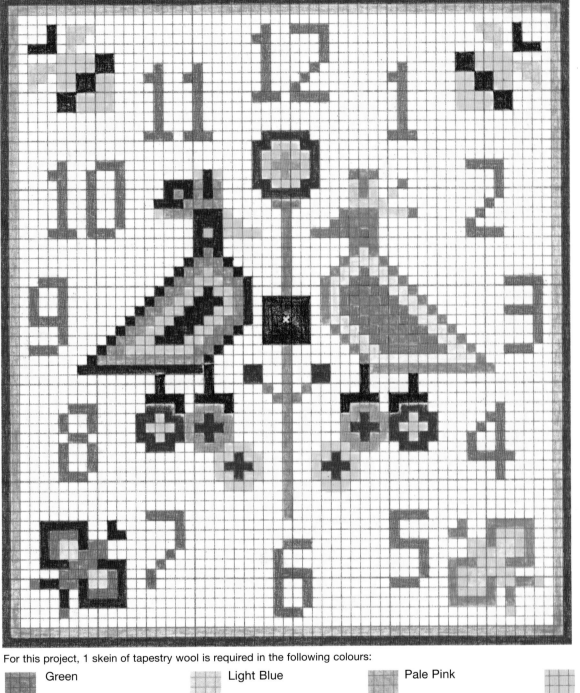

For this project, 1 skein of tapestry wool is required in the following colours:

Green	Light Blue	Pale Pink	Yellow
Black	Royal Blue	Red	
Dark Blue	Purple	Orange	

TEMPLATES

Templates are guides which can be traced around in order to transfer a design onto the object to be decorated. To enlarge the templates to the size that you require, draw a grid of equal-sized squares over your tracing. Measure the space where the shape is to go and then draw a grid to these proportions, with an equal number of squares as appear on your tracing. Take each square individually and draw the relevant parts of the pattern in the larger square. Alternatively, you can enlarge your tracing on a photocopier.

Templates without grids have been reproduced the same size as the project.

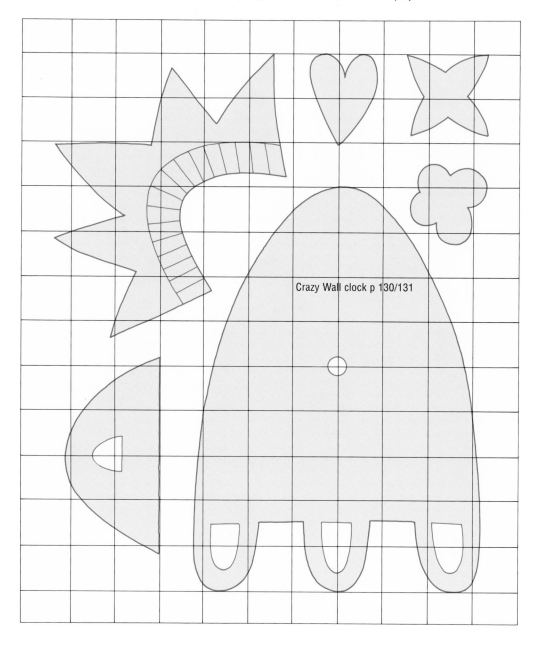

Crazy Wall clock p 130/131

Cat clock p48/49

Gothic clock p24/25

Sunburst
clock p100/1

Dandelion clock p54/55

Mariner's compass clock p44/45

Sunset clock p70/71

Oak leaf clock p88/89

Spider's Web clock p80/81

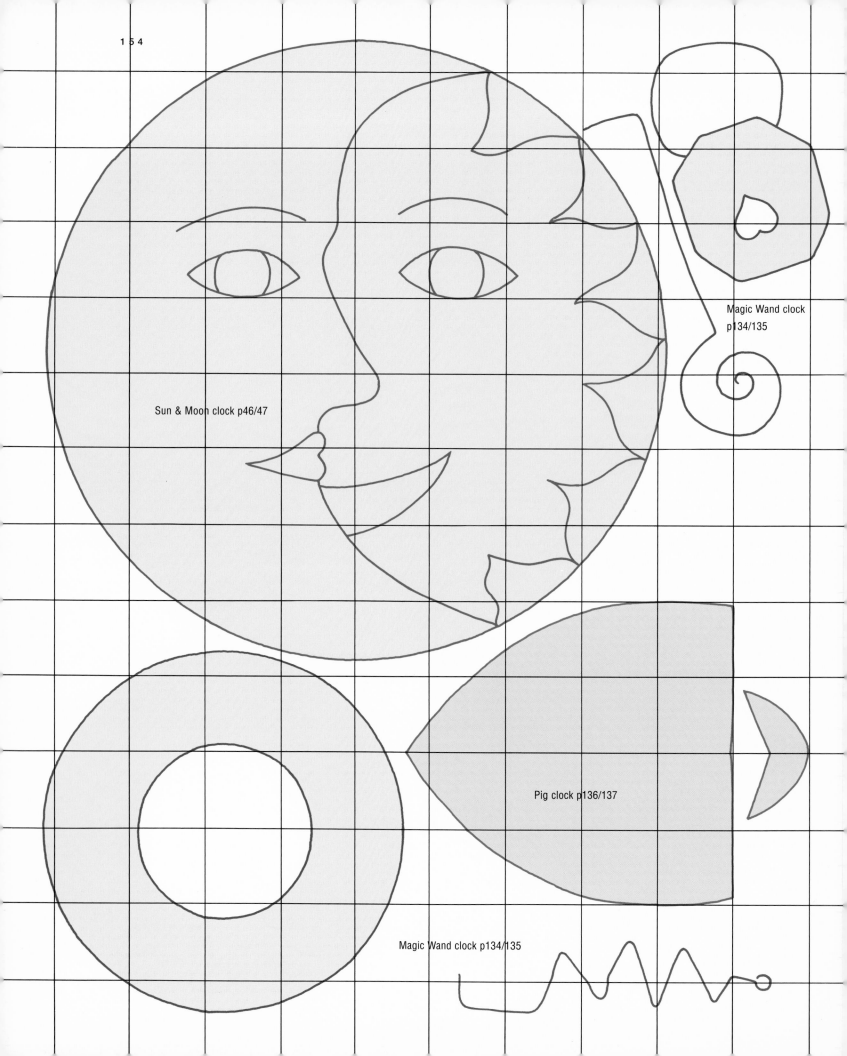

Magic Wand clock p134/135

Sun & Moon clock p46/47

Pig clock p136/137

Magic Wand clock p134/135

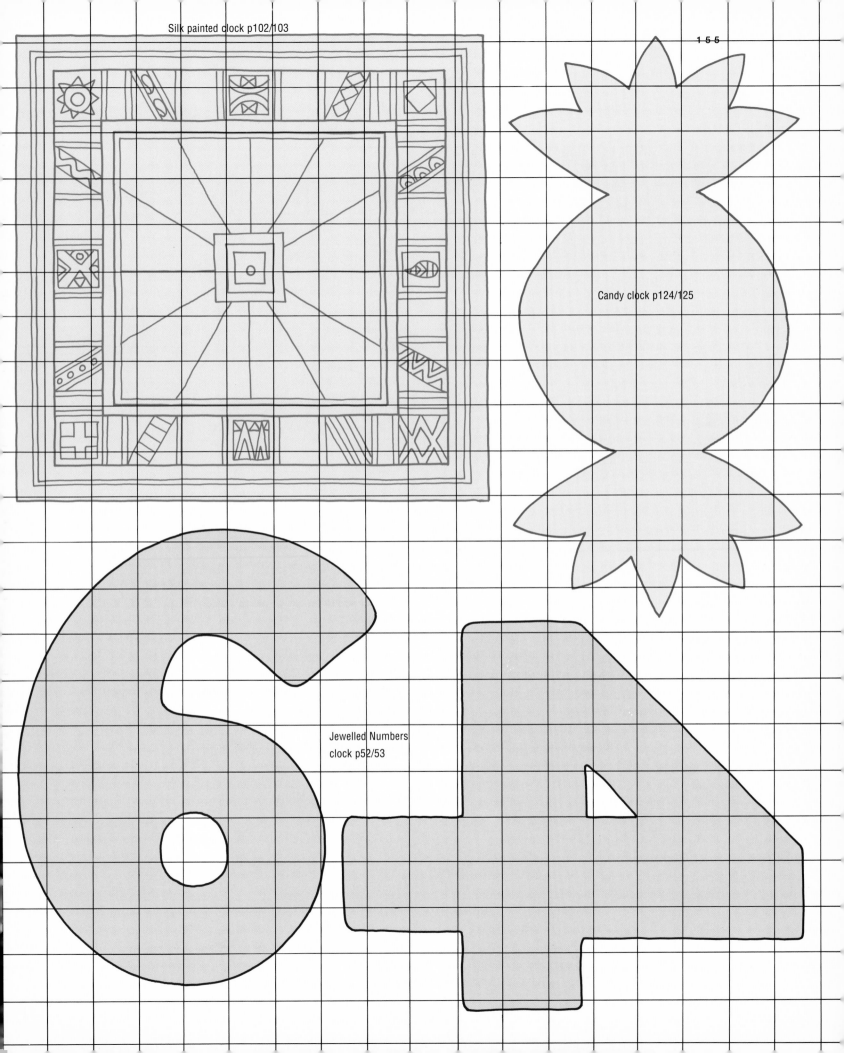

Silk painted clock p102/103

1 5 5

Candy clock p124/125

Jewelled Numbers
clock p52/53

Grandfather clock p64/65

Mantel clock p66/67

Pressed Flower clock p86/87

CONTRIBUTORS

The Publishers would like to thank the following contributors for projects reproduced within this book.

OFER ACOO (Gothic and Magic Wand Clocks) trained in Fine Art and Graphic Design, specialising in concept design for magazines. She now designs and makes unusual art interior and fashion accessories.

AMANDA BLUNDEN (Grandfather Clock) is a specialist in papier-mâché. Trained in Fine Art, her folk-art inspired work is seen in shops, magazines, books and made to commission.

PETRA BOASE (Clay Hearts, Mosaic Tile, Strawberry Salt Dough, Broken China, Driftwood and Tomato Clocks) trained in embroidery and textiles. Her distinctive mixture of bright patterns and colours can be seen widely in books, magazine articles and commercial gift wrap illustration.

CHRIS CONROY (Wood and Plaster Clock) trained as a furniture designer. He produces a range of recycled domestic goods for retail in Japan, Britain and Eire. He continues to experiment with reclaimed materials such as hot glass, steel, copper and timber which he wants to use in the production of quality furniture.

MARY FELLOWS (Jester and Papier-Mâché Wall Clocks) trained in three-dimensional design. She now specializes in ceramics, producing a range of brightly painted interior objects, as well as working to commission.

LUCINDA GANDERTON (Mariner's Compass, Spider's Web, Sunburst and Art Deco Appliqué Clocks) studied embroidery and textiles at Goldsmiths College and is highly sought after as a designer. Lucinda is happy working in most media and has already published books on Salt Dough and Romantic Keepsakes for Lorenz Books.

JILL HANCOCK (Dandelion Clock) is a talented decorative artist specializing in painted wooden toys and nursery furniture. Her use of rich colours and intricate patterns give the work a distinctive style. Her work can be seen in galleries throughout Britain as well as in books, magazines, and top London stores.

RACHEL HOWARD MARSHALL (Bird of Paradise, Raffia Petal, Collage and Pink Pig Clocks) was taught to crochet at the age of 7 by her Czechoslovakian grandmother. Her colourful childhood, much of it on the move, and a passion for the old and new, are the main influences in her work. She specializes in crochet, fashion design and stage costumes, making cloths and accessories to commission.

JACK MOXLEY (Oak Leaf Clock) is a student at Dulwich College and has featured in various books. He is good at mathematics, computing, design and technology.

OLIVER MOXLEY (Jewelled Numbers Clock) is a student at Alleyns School in Dulwich. He has participated in a number of adult and children's books both as a model and a maker, and has appeared on the Learning Channel 'Craftwise' series.

SARBJITT NATT (Silk Painted Clock) is a talented artist who specialises in silk painting. She has written and contributed to many craft books and magazines and undertakes commissions.

KATHERINE REEKIE (Mantel Clock) originally studied Fine Art, later she trained as a carpenter/joiner. Her unusual and imaginative papier-mâché creations reflect the tensions between the practical and fanciful aspects of household objects.

EMMA WHITFIELD (Cat, Heart and Ribbons, Sunset and Découpage Clocks) specializes in the art of découpage, particularly the decorating of hat boxes. Trained in Fine Art, she exhibits at prestigious craft fairs around Britain.

JOSEPHINE WHITFIELD (Sun and Moon, Triple-faced, String and Woodland Clocks) is a specialist in decorated furniture and restoration. She employs her training in fine art to transform everyday objects into pieces of distinctive beauty.

DOROTHY WOOD (Salt Dough Teapot, Windowbox, Pressed Flower, Snakes and Ladders, Needlepoint Octagonal, Cow Jumped Over the Moon and French Knitting Clocks) trained in embroidery and textiles. She contributes regularly to craft magazines and books, working particularly in the areas of embroidery, salt dough and papercrafts.

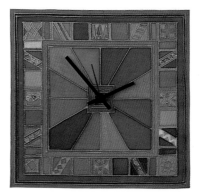

CLOCK SUPPLIERS

The Publishers gratefully acknowledge the following individuals and companies who loaned clocks for the gallery sections, and who would be pleased to accept commissions for clocks.

Mike Abbot and Kim Ellwood, Metal Factory: 39-41 North Road, Islington, London N7 9DP. Tel: 0171 700 0828

Ofer Acoo: 22 Crescent Road, London N8 8AX. Tel: 0181 341 4387

Adject Design: Unit C4, Metropolitan Business Centre, Enfield Road, London N1 5AZ Tel: 00171 241 1220

Peter Atkinson, Alternative Vision: 17 Wilton Road, Muswell Hill, London N10 1LX. Tel: 0181 444 1703

Sally Bourne: c/o 7 + 7 Futons and Interiors, 91 Northcote Road, London SW11 6PL. Tel: 0171 924 1753

Amanda Blunden: 2 Teyham Court, 158 Northcote Road, London SW11 6RG. Tel: 0171 924 7698

Rosie Casseldon, tictoc: 159 Westminster Road, Sutton, Surrey SM1 3NQ. Tel: 0181 641 4007

Chris Conroy, furniture: 31 Reeves Road, Kings Heath, Birmingham B14 5SG. Tel: 0121 624 3339

Gerry Copp: School Cottage, Aisthorpe, Lincoln, LN1 2SG. Tel: 01522 730218

Isobel Dennis, Clockworks Studio: 38 Southwell Road, London SE5 9PG. Tel: 0171 326 1880

Mary Fellows: 401 1/2 Workshops, Wandsworth Road, London SW8 2JP. Tel: 0171 622 7261

Anne Finlay: 7 Bellevue Terrace, Edinburgh EH7 4DT. Tel: 0131 556 3415

Maria Heslop: 28b Yonge Park, Finsbury Park, London N4 3NT. Tel: 0171 607 9416

Bruce Jacobs: 73 Straight Bit, Flackwell Heath, Buckinghamshire HP10 9NG. Tel: 01628 525792

Caroline Kelley: 5 Bowling Green, St Ives, Cornwall TR25 15H Tel: 01736 794042

Kate Long: c/o 7 + 7 Futons and Interiors, 91 Northcote Road, London SW11 6PL. Tel: 0171 924 1753

David Mitchell Design: 63 Charlbert Court, Mackennal Street, London NW8 7DB. Tel: 0171 483 0548

Cheryl Owen: Unit 117, 31 Clerkenwell Close, London EC1 0AT. Tel: 0171 251 1923

Pampas Design: Glanafon, Caenycoed, Llandloes, Powys SY18 6SG. Tel: 01686 412041

Richard Pell, Creative Metalwork: Unit 6 Park Mews, Croxted Road, London SE24 9DB. Tel: 0181 678 0800

Katherine Reekie: 4 Rodwell Road, East Dulwich, London SE22 9LF. Tel: 0181 693 5810

Jenny Robson, Tic Tok Design: 162 Barrow Road, Sileby, Loughborough LE12 7LR. Tel 01509 814803

Ryan Soloman: 376 John Street London EC1V 4NN. Tel: 0171 837 5639

Karen Triffit: Flat 2, 237 South Lambeth Road, London SW8 1XR. Tel: 0171 735 0883

Emma Whitfield: 3 Tressidder House, Poynders Road, London SW4 8PH. Tel: 081 674 5220

Josephine Whitfield: 34 Wilton House, Dog Kennel Hill, East Dulwich, London SE22 8AE. Tel: 0171 733 0668

Ann Wood: Unit 15, The Metropolitan Workshops, Enfield Road, London N1 5AZ. Tel: 0181 340 0956

SUPPLIERS OF CLOCK PARTS

The following companies all supply clock movements, numerals, parts and tools.

UK
Axis Accessories Limited
24a Camden Road
London NW1 9DP

C & L Clocks
Kings Hill Industrial Estate
Bude
Cornwall
EX23 8QN
01288 353351

US
Clock Repair Center
Clocks Parts Movements Numerals Tools
33 Boyd Street

Westbury, New York
1-516-997-4810

Otto Frei and Jules Borel Co
Battery Clock Movements
126 2nd Avenue
Oakland, CA
1-510-832-0355

AUSTRALIA
Cobb & Co Clocks Aust Pty Ltd
Unit 16,
447 Warrigal Road
Moorabbin Vic
03 532 2955

Around the Clock for Clock Parts
186 Queen Street
Campbelltown
Sydney NSW
046 28 4141

Adelaide Clock Movements
6 Surrey Road
Keswick
Adelaide SA
08 297 5933

Wagen Klockraft
2 Clare Court
Winthrop
Perth WA
09 332 5174

Clock Movements Importers
Unit 3018
496 Sherwood Road
Sherwood
Brisban Qld 4075
07 278 2103

NEW ZEALAND
Neal Distributors
4 Botha Road
Penrose
Auckland
09 525 5442

INDEX

PICTURE ACKNOWLEDGEMENTS

The Publishers would like to thank the following picture libraries for permission to reproduce photographs in this book.

E.T. Archive: p 6L & R; p 7R; p9 Bottom L & R.
The Bridgeman Art Library: p 8L & R; p 9 top L; p 10 L & R.
Mary Evans Picture Library: p 7L

MATERIAL SUPPLIERS

The Publisher's gratefully acknowledge the following companies who supplied materials for use in the projects.

French Knitting clock: Bond Cord Maker supplied by Bond Knitting Systems Ltd, Unit 3, TF Smith Buildings, 154 Newland, Witney, Oxon, OX8 6JH.

Stranded Cotton and Cotton Pearl supplied by Coats Patons Crafts, PO Box McMullin Road, Darlington, Co. Durham DL1 1YQ.

Craft Supplies Ltd: The Mill, Millers Dale, Near Buxton, Derbyshire SK17 8SN. Tel: 01298 871636 (mail order and shop)

C & L Clocks Cornwall: Kings Hill Industrial Estate, Bude, Cornwall EX23 8QN.
Tel: 01288 353351 (mail order suppliers of clock parts, hand, pendulums, faces)

Creative Beadcraft: Denmark Works, Sheecote Dell Road, Beamond End, Nr Amersham, Buckinghamshire HP7 0RX. Tel: 01494 715606 (mail order supplier of beads, carbuchons etc.)

Gleave & Co: 111-113 St John Street, Clerkenwell, London EC1V 4JA.
Tel: 0171 253 1345

7 + 7 Futons and Interiors, 91 Northcote Road, London SW11 6PL.
Tel: 0171 924 1753